NINJA CREAMI

Recipe Book

Deliciously Simple Recipes for Ice Creams, Sorbets, Gelatos, smoothie bowls, milkshakes, sauces, toppings, and mix-ins for Beginners and Advanced Users

Sophie Stuart

Introduction

Whether you're a novice in the kitchen or a seasoned chef, the Ninja CREAMi Recipe book is your ultimate guide to creating homemade frozen masterpieces that will impress your family and friends.

From creamy ice creams and refreshing sorbets to rich gelatos and vibrant smoothie bowls, there's something for everyone.

This book will walk you through the process of making ice cream, sorbet, smoothie bowls and milkshakes step by step (I promise you'll be amazed at how quickly it comes together).

How the Ninja Creami works

At the touch of a button, the Ninja CREAMi transforms frozen solid bases into ice cream, sorbets, milkshakes, and smoothie bowls.

The Creami uses Ninja's Creamify technology to break down a uniformly frozen block into a super smooth, creamy texture in just 3 minutes.

Creamerizer Paddle:
The Creamerizer Paddle aids in the transformation of frozen ingredients into creamy, tasty texture treats.

How to use Ninja Creami?

You'll need to prepare the base ahead of time, To make the base, simply combine the ingredients of your favourite ice cream, sorbet, or milkshake recipe from this book, blend, and freeze overnight. Once completely frozen, place the frozen pint in outer bowl, screw on the paddle lid, and load it into the machine. Finally, select the option for the type of dessert you're making, and you'll have a tub of freshly made ice cream, sorbet, or smoothie bowl in less than 3 minutes.

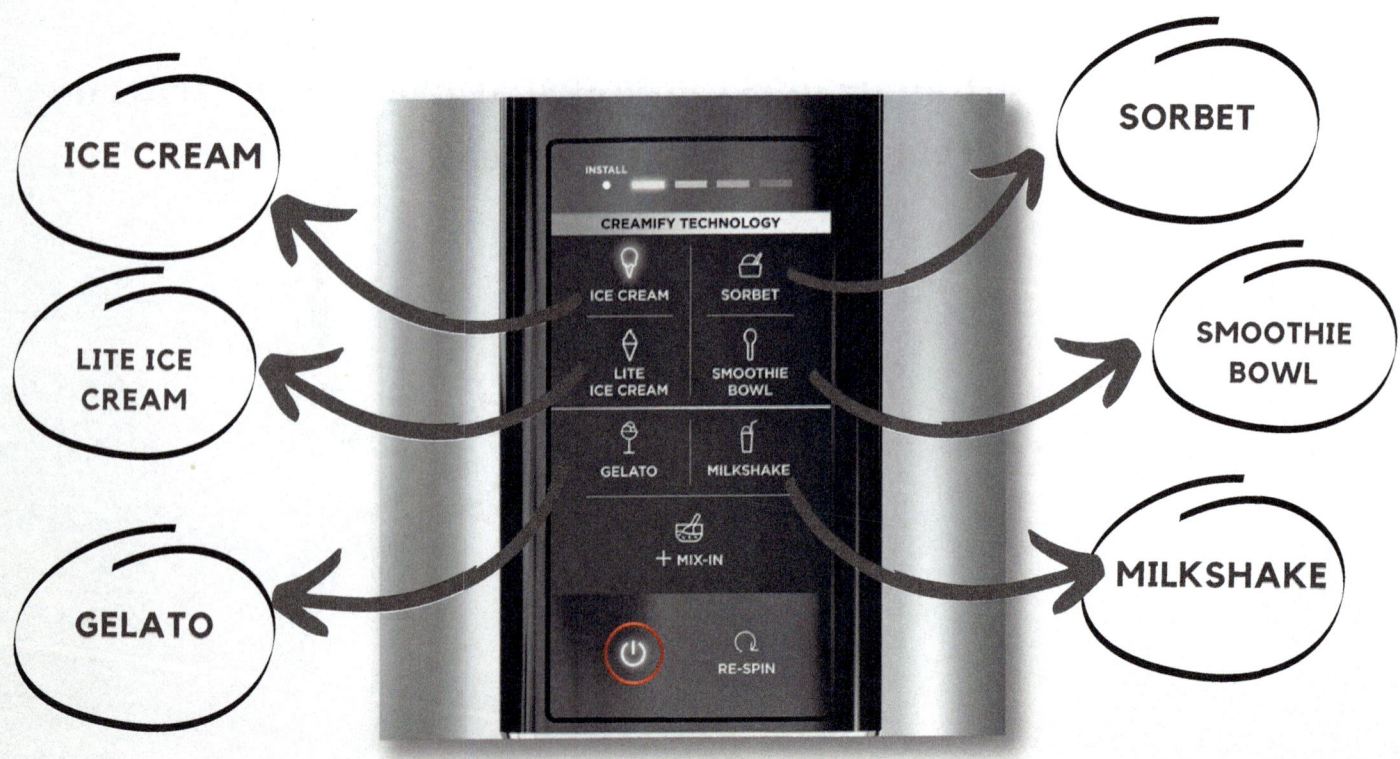

ICE CREAM

LITE ICE CREAM

GELATO

SORBET

SMOOTHIE BOWL

MILKSHAKE

How to Turn recipes in This book to Dairy-free, Sugar-free, or Egg-free ?

Replacing Dairy:

If you're lactose intolerant, following a keto diet or vegan but don't want to give up ice cream, you're not alone. Here are some dairy substitutes that you can use.

If an allergy or intolerance is the reason for avoiding dairy, the replacement alternatives can be lactose-free milk and/or cream, which may typically be used in the same way as "regular" milk and cream.

- Soy milk, rice milk, almond milk, almond-cashew milk, and coconut milk can be substituted for regular milk. Substitute at a one-to-one ratio for what is listed in the recipe.

- If you do need a a dairy-free cream to whip up like a traditional double cream, then this is the best method for you. It is also the most simple substitute! All you will need for this option is a tin of coconut cream. Substitute at a one-to-one ratio for what is listed in the recipe.

Replacing Eggs:

You could be vegan, allergic to eggs, or just plain afraid of eggs. Don't worry. There is a way to stay very close to your original recipe without using eggs. Instead, we'll use cornflour.

- To make egg-less Gelato with cornflour, follow the same steps as you would to make a 'regular' Gelato base. However, instead of eggs, you thicken the base with cornflour. Making a custard this way is simple, and it is less likely to overcook or split!

- Use 2 tablespoons of cornflour plus 3 tablespoons of liquid for every egg you need to replace.

- Cornflour thickens only when heated. To make the custard, first combine the cornflour and liquids, then heat the mixture. The starches gelatinize and thicken the base as it heats.

Replacing Sugar:

The ice cream will be made in the same way as usual, with the exception that the sugar is replaced by sweeteners.

Ice Cream

STRAWBERRY CHEESECAKE ICE CREAM

Serving size 4   **Prep time 5 mins**

INGREDIENTS

- 30g cream cheese, softened
- 55g caster sugar
- 1 tsp vanilla extract
- 150ml double cream
- 230ml milk
- 200g fresh strawberries, trimmed, cut in quarters
- 50g crushed butter cookies or pretzel, for mix-in

DIRECTIONS

1. In a bowl, add all ingredients (except cookies). Whisk until combined.
2. Pour mixture into Ninja Creami tub container, ensuring it does not go over the max fill line. Freeze the tub for 24 hours.
3. After 24 hours, remove the tub from the freezer, and plug in your Ninja Creami.
4. Remove the lid from the tub and grab Ninja Creami outer bowl. Place tub securely into the outer bowl and cover with lid. Once lid is on, place the outer bowl into the machine, twisting to the right until it locks into place. Press the "Ice Cream" button.
5. Twist the lid off of the outer bowl and remove the tub.
6. With a spoon, create a 4cm wide hole that reaches the bottom of the tub. Add the cookies to the hole and process again using the MIX-IN program.
7. Once processing is complete, remove ice cream from tub and serve immediately.

CRANBERRY FROZEN YOGURT

Serving size 4   **Prep time 5 mins**

INGREDIENTS

- 90ml yogurt
- 135ml double cream
- 135ml milk
- 70g caster sugar
- 1 tsp vanilla extract
- 2 tbsp honey
- 200g fresh or frozen cranberries

Mix-in ideas:
- 50g chopped toasted pecans, or
- 50g white chocolate chips
- 50g Chopped candied ginger

DIRECTIONS

1. In a bowl, add all ingredients (except cranberries). Whisk until combined.
2. Pour mixture into Ninja Creami tub container, ensuring it does not go over the max fill line. Add the cranberries. Freeze the tub for 24 hours.
3. After 24 hours, remove the tub from the freezer, and plug in your Ninja Creami.
4. Remove the lid from the tub and grab Ninja Creami outer bowl. Place tub securely into the outer bowl and cover with lid. Once lid is on, place the outer bowl into the machine, twisting to the right until it locks into place. Press the "Ice Cream" button
5. Once processing is complete, remove yogurt from tub and serve immediately.

LIME PIE ICE CREAM

Serving size 4   **Prep time** 5 mins

INGREDIENTS

- 100ml fresh squeezed and strained lime juice
- 120ml sweetened condensed milk
- 200ml double cream
- 1 tsp lime zest
- 1-2 drops green food coloring (optional)
- 50g crushed vanilla cookies, for mix-in

DIRECTIONS

1. In a bowl, add all ingredients (except cookies). Whisk until combined.
2. Pour mixture into Ninja Creami tub container, ensuring it does not go over the max fill line. Freeze the tub for 24 hours.
3. After 24 hours, remove the tub from the freezer, and plug in your Ninja Creami.
4. Remove the lid from the tub and grab Ninja Creami outer bowl. Place tub securely into the outer bowl and cover with lid. Once lid is on, place the outer bowl into the machine, twisting to the right until it locks into place. Press the "Ice Cream" button.
5. Twist the lid off of the outer bowl and remove the tub.
6. With a spoon, create a 4cm wide hole that reaches the bottom of the tub. Add the cookies to the hole and process again using the MIX-IN program.
7. Once processing is complete, remove ice cream from tub and serve immediately.

Variations:

- **For Lime Avocado Ice Cream:** add 1 small sliced ripe avocado to the ice cream base mixture
- **For Lime Mint Ice Cream:** Add 1 tbsp chopped fresh mint leaves to the lime ice cream base

RASPBERRY THYME GELATO

Serving size 4   **Prep time** 10 mins

INGREDIENTS

- 230ml double cream
- 180ml milk
- 230g raspberries
- 70g caster sugar
- 4 egg yolks
- 1 tsp vanilla extract
- 2 tbsp chopped, fresh thyme leaves

DIRECTIONS

1. Place the raspberries, and vanilla in a blender and puree until smooth. Set aside.
2. In a saucepan, add milk, thyme, cream, sugar, egg yolk and whisk until combined.
3. Place the saucepan on hop over medium heat. Heat the mixture, stirring occasionally, until it reaches a 74-79°C. Remove from heat.
4. Strain mixture through a fine-mesh sieve into an empty tub, ensuring it does not go over the max fill line. Place tub into an ice bath. Once cooled, add the pureed raspberries and stir, place lid on tub and freeze for at least 24 hours.
5. After 24 hours, remove the tub from the freezer and remove lid from tub, and let it thaw for 5 minutes. Place the tub in the Creami and lock the lid. Select GELATO.
6. Once processing is complete,remove gelato from tub . Serve immediately.

APRICOT FROZEN YOGURT

Serving size 4   **Prep time** 5 mins

INGREDIENTS

- 90ml plain yogurt
- 135ml double cream
- 135ml milk
- 70g sugar
- 1 tsp lemon zest
- 100g apricots, chopped
- 1 tsp vanilla extract
- 1 tbsp lemon juice

DIRECTIONS

1. In a bowl, add all ingredients (except apricots). Whisk until combined.
2. Pour mixture into Ninja Creami tub container, ensuring it does not go over the max fill line. Add the apricots. Freeze the tub for 24 hours.
3. After 24 hours, remove the tub from the freezer, and plug in your Ninja Creami.
4. Remove the lid from the tub and grab Ninja Creami outer bowl. Place tub securely into the outer bowl and cover with lid. Once lid is on, place the outer bowl into the machine, twisting to the right until it locks into place. Press the "Ice Cream" button
5. Once processing is complete, remove yogurt from tub and serve immediately.

- **Add Chopped pistachios as a mix-in** for a vibrant green color and a slightly salty flavor that complements the apricot yogurt.

MIXED BERRY ICE CREAM

Serving size 4   **Prep time 5 mins**

INGREDIENTS

- 225g fresh or frozen mixed berries
- Pinch of salt   • 250ml double cream
- 55g sugar   • 70g frozen berries, for mix-in

DIRECTIONS

1. In a bowl, add all ingredients (except mix-ins) and mix until combined.
2. Pour base into an empty tub, ensuring it does not go over the max fill line. Place lid on tub and freeze for 24 hours.
3. After 24 hours, remove the tub from the freezer and remove lid from tub, and let it thaw for 5 minutes. Place the tub in the Creami and lock the lid. Select ICE CREAM.
4. Twist the lid off of the outer bowl and remove the tub.
5. With a spoon, create a 4cm wide hole that reaches the bottom of the tub. Add the mix-in to the hole and process again using the MIX-IN program.
6. Once processing is complete, remove ice cream from tub and serve immediately.

- **Add chopped candied nuts as a mix-in,** such as pecans or almonds, for a crunchy and sweet element.

MANGO KULFI

Serving size 4   **Prep time 4 mins**

INGREDIENTS

- 120g fresh or frozen mango chucks
- 100g condensed milk   • ½ tsp vanilla extract
- 180ml double cream   • ½ tsp Cardamom powder

DIRECTIONS

1. In a bowl, add all ingredients (except mango). Whisk until combined.
2. Pour mixture into Ninja Creami tub container, ensuring it does not go over the max fill line. Add the mango. Freeze the tub for 24 hours.
3. After 24 hours, remove the tub from the freezer, and plug in your Ninja Creami.
4. Remove the lid from the tub and grab Ninja Creami outer bowl. Place tub securely into the outer bowl and cover with lid. Once lid is on, place the outer bowl into the machine, twisting to the right until it locks into place. Press the "Ice Cream" button
5. Once processing is complete, remove yogurt from tub and serve immediately.

KIWI ICE CREAM

Serving size 4   **Prep time 4 mins**

INGREDIENTS

- 6 kiwis, peeled and mashed
- 80g sugar
- 250ml double cream

DIRECTIONS

1. In a bowl, add all ingredients. Whisk until combined.
2. Pour mixture into Ninja Creami tub container, ensuring it does not go over the max fill line. Freeze the tub for 24 hours.
3. After 24 hours, remove the tub from the freezer, and plug in your Ninja Creami.
4. Remove the lid from the tub and grab Ninja Creami outer bowl. Place tub securely into the outer bowl and cover with lid. Once lid is on, place the outer bowl into the machine, twisting to the right until it locks into place. Press the "Ice Cream" button
5. Once processing is complete, remove yogurt from tub and serve immediately

Variations:
- **For Mint kiwi ice cream:** add 1 tbsp fresh chopped mint leaves to the ice cream base
- **For Coconut kiwi ice cream:** use coconut milk in place of some of the double cream.

LEMON ICE CREAM

Serving size 4   **Prep time 4 mins**

INGREDIENTS

- 250ml double cream
- 100ml milk
- 100g sugar
- 1 tbsp lemon zest
- 120ml fresh lemon juice
- A drop or two of food coloring

DIRECTIONS

1. In a bowl, add all ingredients. Mix until sugar dissolved.
2. Pour base into an empty tub, ensuring it does not go over the max fill line. Place lid on tub and freeze for 24 hours.
3. After 24 hours, remove the tub from the freezer and remove lid from tub, and let it thaw for 5 minutes. Place the tub in the Creami and lock the lid. Select ICE CREAM.
4. Once the process is finished, ice cream is ready to enjoy.

BANANA COCONUT FROZEN YOGURT

Serving size 4   **Prep time** 5 mins

INGREDIENTS

- 90ml yogurt
- 135ml double cream
- 135ml coconut milk
- Pinch of salt
- 1 large ripe bananas, sliced
- 70g sugar

DIRECTIONS

1. In a bowl, add all ingredients (except banana). Whisk until combined.
2. Pour mixture into Ninja Creami tub container, ensuring it does **not go over the max fill** line. Add the banana slices. Freeze the tub for 24 hours.
3. After 24 hours, remove the tub from the freezer, and plug in your Ninja Creami.
4. Remove the lid from the tub and grab Ninja Creami outer bowl. Place tub securely into the outer bowl and cover with lid. Once lid is on, place the outer bowl into the machine, twisting to the right until it locks into place. Press the "Ice Cream" button
5. Once processing is complete, remove yogurt from tub and serve immediately.

Combine toasted coconut flakes with chopped toasted almonds and sprinkle the mixture over the frozen yogurt for a tropical and nutty topping.

LEMON BLUEBERRY FROZEN YOGURT

Serving size 4   **Prep time** 5 mins

INGREDIENTS

- 90ml plain yogurt
- 135ml double cream
- 135ml milk
- 70g sugar
- 1 tbsp lemon juice
- 1 tsp lemon zest
- 50g frozen blueberries, for mix-in

DIRECTIONS

1. In a bowl, add all ingredients (except frozen blueberries). Whisk **until combined.**
2. Pour mixture into an empty tub, ensuring it does not go over the **max fill line. Place lid** on tub and freeze for 24 hours.
3. After 24 hours, remove the tub from the freezer and remove lid f**rom tub, and let it thaw** for 5 minutes. Place the tub in the Creami and lock the lid. Select ICE CREAM.
4. Twist the lid off of the outer bowl and remove the tub.
5. With a spoon, create a 4cm wide hole that reaches the bottom of the tub. Add the frozen blueberries to the hole and process again using the MIX-IN program.
6. Once the process is finished, ice cream is ready to enjoy.

ROASTED FIG ICE CREAM

Serving size 4   **Prep time 20 mins**

INGREDIENTS

- 200g fresh figs
- 225ml double cream
- 140ml milk
- 30g soft cream cheese
- 70g sugar
- juice of 1 lemon

Some mix-in ideas you can try:
- Crushed gingerbread cookies
- Chopped toasted almonds
- Chopped dates

DIRECTIONS

1. Preheat oven to 200C.
2. Slice figs in half and place them cut side up, on a baking sheet. Roast for 15 minutes.
3. In a blender, add roasted figs and all ingredients blend until smooth.
4. Pour mixture into an empty tub, ensuring it does not go over the max fill line. Place lid on tub and freeze for 24 hours.
5. After 24 hours, remove the tub from the freezer and remove lid from tub, and let it thaw for 5 minutes. Place the tub in the Creami and lock the lid. Select ICE CREAM.
6. Twist the lid off of the outer bowl and remove the tub.
7. With a spoon, create a 4cm wide hole that reaches the bottom of the tub. Add the Mix-In to the hole and process again using the MIX-IN program.
8. Once the process is finished, ice cream is ready to enjoy.

CHERRY ICE CREAM

Serving size 4   **Prep time 10 mins**

INGREDIENTS

- 225g cherries, pitted and cut into half
- 80g sugar
- 260ml double cream

DIRECTIONS

1. In a bowl, add cherries, sugar, and mash with a fork. **Add remaining ingredients and mix until combined.**
2. Pour mixture into an empty tub, ensuring it does not go over the max fill line. Place lid on tub and freeze for 24 hours.
3. After 24 hours, remove the tub from the freezer and remove lid from tub, and let it thaw for 5 minutes. Place the tub in the Creami and lock the lid. Select ICE CREAM.
4. Once processing is complete, remove ice cream from tub and serve immediately.

For a quick chocolate sauce topping, heat 120ml double cream until simmering, remove from heat and then add 90g chocolate chips, 2 tbsp butter, 2 tbsp sugar, and 1 tsp vanilla extract. Stir until smooth and drizzle over ice cream.

BLOOD ORANGE ICE CREAM

Serving size 4 **Prep time 5 mins**

INGREDIENTS

- 250ml double cream
- 100ml milk
- 80g sugar
- 120ml blood orange juice or regular orange juice
- A drop or two of food coloring

DIRECTIONS

1. In a bowl, add all ingredients. Mix until sugar dissolved.
2. Pour base into an empty tub, ensuring it does not go over the max fill line. Place lid on tub and freeze for 24 hours.
3. After 24 hours, remove the tub from the freezer and remove lid from tub, and let it thaw for 5 minutes. Place the tub in the Creami and lock the lid. Select ICE CREAM.
4. Once the process is finished, ice cream is ready to enjoy.

PEAR ICE CREAM

Serving size 4 **Prep time 5 mins**

INGREDIENTS

- 120ml milk
- 150ml double cream
- 1 tsp cinnamon powder
- 225g ripe pears, peeled, cored and sliced
- 80g sugar

DIRECTIONS

1. In a blender, add all ingredients. Blend until smooth.
2. Pour base into an empty tub, ensuring it does not go over the max fill line. Place lid on tub and freeze for 24 hours.
3. After 24 hours, remove the tub from the freezer and remove lid from tub, and let it thaw for 5 minutes. Place the tub in the Creami and lock the lid. Select ICE CREAM.
4. Once the process is finished, ice cream is ready to enjoy.

PINEAPPLE COCONUT ICE CREAM

Serving size 4   **Prep time 5 mins**

INGREDIENTS

- 400ml coconut milk
- 100g sugar
- 230g frozen pineapple

DIRECTIONS

1. In a blender, add coconut milk, pineapple and sugar. Blend until very smooth.
2. Pour base into an empty tub, ensuring it does not go over the max fill line. Place lid on tub and freeze for 24 hours.
3. After 24 hours, remove the tub from the freezer and remove lid from tub, and let it thaw for 5 minutes. Place the tub in the Creami and lock the lid. Select ICE CREAM.
4. Once the process is finished, ice cream is ready to enjoy.

STRAWBERRY GELATO

Serving size 4   **Prep time 10 mins**

INGREDIENTS

- 230ml double cream
- 180ml milk
- 230g strawberries (stems and hulls removed)
- 70g sugar
- 4 egg yolks
- 1 tsp vanilla extract

DIRECTIONS

1. Place the strawberries, and vanilla in a blender and puree until smooth. Set aside.
2. In a saucepan, add milk, cream, sugar, egg yolk and whisk until combined.
3. Place the saucepan on hop over medium heat. Heat the mixture, stirring occasionally, until it reaches a 74-79°C. Remove from heat.
4. Strain mixture through a fine-mesh sieve into an empty tub, ensuring it does not go over the max fill line. Place tub into an ice bath. Once cooled, add the pureed strawberry and stir, place lid on tub and freeze for at least 24 hours.
5. After 24 hours, remove the tub from the freezer and remove lid from tub, and let it thaw for 5 minutes. Place the tub in the Creami and lock the lid. Select GELATO.
6. Once processing is complete,remove gelato from tub . Serve immediately.

Add a refreshing touch by drizzling mint-infused chocolate sauce over the gelato. Heat 150ml double cream with 100g chocolate until melted, then stir in 1/2 tsp peppermint extract.

BASIL GELATO

Serving size 4   **Prep time** 10 mins

INGREDIENTS

- 230ml double cream
- 180ml milk
- 4 egg yolks
- 80g caster sugar
- 16 basil leaves
- Pinch of salt
- 1 tbsp lemon extract
- 6 drops green food coloring (optional)

DIRECTIONS

1. In a saucepan, add all ingredients and whisk until combined.
2. Place the saucepan on hop over medium heat. Heat the mixture, **stirring occasionally,** until it reaches a 74-79°C. Remove from heat.
3. Strain mixture through a fine-mesh sieve into an empty tub, ensuring it does not go over the max fill line. Place tub into an ice bath. Once cooled, place lid on tub and freeze for at least 24 hours.
4. After 24 hours, remove the tub from the freezer and remove lid from tub, and let it thaw for 5 minutes. Place the tub in the Creami and lock the lid. Select GELATO.
5. Once processing is complete, remove gelato from tub . Serve the basil gelato scoops with fresh basil leaves for garnish.

AVOCADO ICE CREAM

Serving size 4   **Prep time** 5 mins

INGREDIENTS

- 3 medium ripe avocados
- 100g sugar
- 1 tsp golden syrup/honey
- 1 tsp lemon juice
- 250ml double cream
- 70g dark Chocolate chips, for mix-in

DIRECTIONS

1. Scoop the avocados insides into a blender. Add sugar, honey, double cream, lemon juice. Puree until smooth.
2. Pour base into an empty tub, ensuring it does not go over the max fill line. Place lid on tub and freeze for 24 hours.
3. After 24 hours, remove the tub from the freezer and remove lid from tub, and let it thaw for 5 minutes. Place the tub in the Creami and lock the lid. Select ICE CREAM.
4. Twist the lid off of the outer bowl and remove the tub.
5. With a spoon, create a 4cm wide hole that reaches the bottom of the tub. Add the chocolate chips to the hole and process again using the MIX-IN program.
6. Once processing is complete, remove ice cream from tub and serve immediately.

LEMON BLUEBERRY CHEESECAKE ICE CREAM

Serving size 4   **Prep time 5 mins**

INGREDIENTS

- 30g cream cheese, softened
- 60g sugar
- 150ml double cream
- 230ml milk
- 1 tsp vanilla extract
- 1 tbsp lemon juice
- 1 tsp lemon zest

Blueberry Sauce:
- 225g blueberries
- 50g sugar

DIRECTIONS

1. In a small saucepan, add blueberries and 50g sugar. Boil for 8 minutes, until thickened. Cool completely.
2. In a bowl, add cream cheese and sugar. Whisk until smooth. Add the cream, milk, vanilla, lemon juice, and zest, whisk again until combined.
3. Pour base into an empty tub, ensuring it does not go over the max fill line. Place lid on tub and freeze for 24 hours.
4. After 24 hours, remove the tub from the freezer and remove lid from tub, and let it thaw for 5 minutes. Place the tub in the Creami and lock the lid. Select ICE CREAM.
5. Twist the lid off of the outer bowl and remove the tub.
6. When processing is complete, remove ice cream from tub and serve immediately, topped with blueberry sauce.

RASPBERRY ICE CREAM

Serving size 4   **Prep time 5 mins**

INGREDIENTS

- 230ml milk
- 150ml double cream
- 70g sugar
- 30g cream cheese
- 2 tbsp raspberry jam
- 60g fresh raspberries
- 50g fresh raspberries, cut in half, for mix-in

DIRECTIONS

1. In a bowl, add all ingredients (except mix-ins) and mix until combined.
2. Pour base into an empty tub, ensuring it does not go over the max fill line. Place lid on tub and freeze for 24 hours.
3. After 24 hours, remove the tub from the freezer and remove lid from tub, and let it thaw for 5 minutes. Place the tub in the Creami and lock the lid. Select ICE CREAM.
4. Twist the lid off of the outer bowl and remove the tub.
5. With a spoon, create a 4cm wide hole that reaches the bottom of the tub. Add the raspberries to the hole and process again using the MIX-IN program.
6. Once processing is complete, remove ice cream from tub and serve immediately.
7. Raspberry Pavlova ice cream: swap the frozen raspberries and add 50g broken up meringue for mix-in

For Raspberry Pavlova ice cream: swap the frozen raspberries and add 50g broken up meringue for mix-in.

CRYSTALLISED GINGER ICE CREAM

Serving size 4   **Prep time 5 mins**

INGREDIENTS

- 230ml double cream
- 150ml milk
- 4 tbsp sugar
- 1/4 tsp grated fresh ginger
- 50g chopped crystallised ginger, for mix-in

DIRECTIONS

1. In a bowl, add all ingredients (except crystallised ginger) and mix until combined.
2. Pour base into an empty tub, ensuring it does not go over the max fill line. Place lid on tub and freeze for 24 hours.
3. After 24 hours, remove the tub from the freezer and remove lid from tub, and let it thaw for 5 minutes. Place the tub in the Creami and lock the lid. Select ICE CREAM.
4. Twist the lid off of the outer bowl and remove the tub.
5. With a spoon, create a 4cm wide hole that reaches the bottom of the tub. Add the crystallised ginger to the hole and process again using the MIX-IN program.
6. Once processing is complete, remove ice cream from tub and serve immediately.

LEMON MINT ICE CREAM

Serving size 4   **Prep time 5 mins**

INGREDIENTS

- 150ml double cream
- 100ml milk
- 100g sugar
- 120ml fresh lemon juice
- 1/2 tsp peppermint extract
- 2 or 3 drops yellow food coloring (optional)

DIRECTIONS

1. In a bowl, add all ingredients. Mix until sugar dissolved.
2. Pour base into an empty tub, ensuring it does not go over the max fill line. Place lid on tub and freeze for 24 hours.
3. After 24 hours, remove the tub from the freezer and remove lid from tub, and let it thaw for 5 minutes. Place the tub in the Creami and lock the lid. Select ICE CREAM.
4. Once the process is finished, ice cream is ready to enjoy.

PUMPKIN ICE CREAM

Serving size 4   **Prep time** 10 mins

INGREDIENTS

- 240ml double cream
- 120ml Milk
- 80g sugar
- Pinch Salt
- 1 tsp Vanilla extract
- 120g Pumpkin puree
- 1 ½ tsp Pumpkin spice

DIRECTIONS

1. In a bowl, add all ingredients. Blend until all the sugar is **dissolved**.
2. Pour base into an empty tub, ensuring it does not go over the max fill line. Place lid on tub and freeze for 24 hours.
3. After 24 hours, remove the tub from the freezer and remove lid from tub, and let it thaw for 5 minutes. Place the tub in the Creami and lock the lid. Select ICE CREAM.
4. Once the process is finished, ice cream is ready to enjoy.

VANILLA GELATO

Serving size 4   **Prep time** 15 mins

INGREDIENTS

- 230ml double cream
- 180ml milk
- 4 egg yolks
- 80g caster sugar
- 2 tsp vanilla extract

Some mix-in ideas you can try:
- Crushed cookies
- Chopped toasted nuts
- Brownie chunks
- Candied ginger
- Frozen fruits
- Sprinkles

DIRECTIONS

1. In a saucepan, add milk, cream, vanilla, sugar, egg yolk and whisk until combined.
2. Place the saucepan on hop over medium heat. Heat the mixture, stirring occasionally, until it reaches a 74-79°C. Remove from heat.
3. Strain mixture through a fine-mesh sieve into an empty tub, ensuring it does not go over the max fill line. Place tub into an ice bath. Once cooled, place lid on tub and freeze for at least 24 hours.
4. After 24 hours, remove the tub from the freezer and remove lid from tub, and let it thaw for 5 minutes. Place the tub in the Creami and lock the lid. Select GELATO.
5. Twist the lid off of the outer bowl and remove the tub.
6. With a spoon, create a 4cm wide hole that reaches the bottom of the tub. Add your favourite Mix-in to the and process again using the MIX-IN program.
7. Once processing is complete, remove ice cream from tub and serve immediately.

PEANUT BUTTER ICE CREAM

Serving size 4   **Prep time** 15 mins

INGREDIENTS

- 120ml milk
- 240ml double cream
- 70g sugar
- 120g creamy peanut butter
- 1 tsp vanilla extract
- 1 tsp salt
- 50g mini peanut butter cups or pecans, chopped, for mix-in

DIRECTIONS

1. In a bowl, add all ingredients (except mix-ins) and mix until combined.
2. Pour base into an empty tub, ensuring it does not go over the max fill line. Place lid on tub and freeze for 24 hours.
3. After 24 hours, remove the tub from the freezer and remove lid from tub, and let it thaw for 5 minutes. Place the tub in the Creami and lock the lid. Select ICE CREAM.
4. Twist the lid off of the outer bowl and remove the tub.
5. With a spoon, create a 4cm wide hole that reaches the bottom of the tub. Add the peanut butter cups to the hole and process again using the MIX-IN program.
6. Once processing is complete, remove ice cream from tub and serve immediately.

Mix in crushed pretzels for a sweet and salty crunch.

PEANUT BUTTER, BANANA, & JELLY ICE CREAM

Serving size 4   **Prep time** 5 mins

INGREDIENTS

- 1 large ripe banana, sliced
- 4 tbsp creamy peanut butter
- 100ml milk
- 200ml double cream
- 80g strawberry jam

DIRECTIONS

1. In a bowl, add all ingredients. Mix.
2. Pour base into an empty tub, ensuring it does not go over the max fill line. Place lid on tub and freeze for 24 hours.
3. After 24 hours, remove the tub from the freezer and remove lid from tub, and let it thaw for 5 minutes. Place the tub in the Creami and lock the lid. Select ICE CREAM.
4. Once the process is finished, ice cream is ready to enjoy.

BUTTER PECAN GELATO

Serving size 4   **Prep time** 10 mins

INGREDIENTS

- 230ml double cream
- 180ml milk
- 4 egg yolks
- 80g brown sugar
- 70g chopped pecans, for mix-in

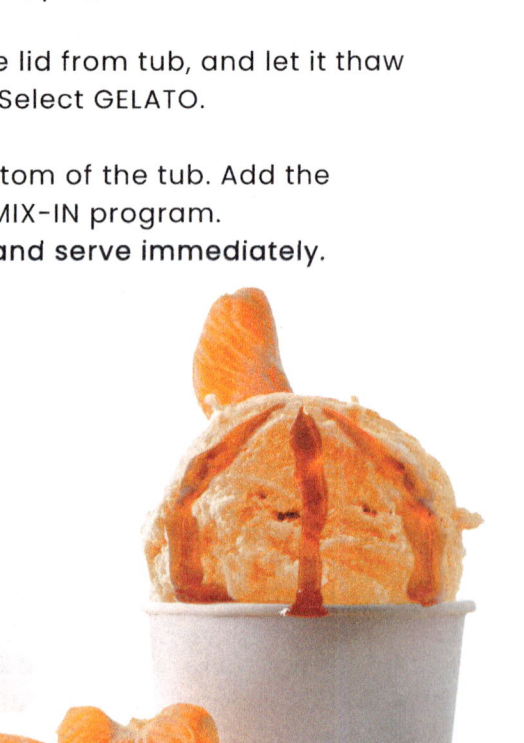

DIRECTIONS

1. In a saucepan, add milk, cream, sugar, egg yolk and whisk until combined.
2. Place the saucepan on hop over medium heat. Heat the mixture, stirring occasionally, until it reaches a 74-79°C. Remove from heat.
3. Strain mixture through a fine-mesh sieve into an empty tub, ensuring it does not go over the max fill line. Place tub into an ice bath. Once cooled, place lid on tub and freeze for at least 24 hours.
4. After 24 hours, remove the tub from the freezer and remove lid from tub, and let it thaw for 5 minutes. Place the tub in the Creami and lock the lid. Select GELATO.
5. Twist the lid off of the outer bowl and remove the tub.
6. With a spoon, create a 4cm wide hole that reaches the bottom of the tub. Add the chopped pecans to the hole and process again using the MIX-IN program.
7. Once processing is complete, remove ice cream from tub and serve immediately.

MANDARIN ICE CREAM

Serving size 4   **Prep time** 6 mins

INGREDIENTS

- 225g fresh or canned Mandarin
- 50ml milk
- 55g caster sugar
- 250ml double cream

DIRECTIONS

1. In a bowl, add all ingredients (except Mandarin). Whisk until combined.
2. Pour mixture into Ninja Creami tub container, ensuring it does not go over the max fill line. Add the Mandarin. Freeze the tub for 24 hours.
3. After 24 hours, remove the tub from the freezer, and plug in your Ninja Creami.
4. Remove the lid from the tub and grab Ninja Creami outer bowl. Place tub securely into the outer bowl and cover with lid. Once lid is on, place the outer bowl into the machine, twisting to the right until it locks into place. Press the "Ice Cream" button
5. Once processing is complete, remove ice cream from tub and serve immediately.

MAPLE WALNUT ICE CREAM

Serving size 4   **Prep time 5 mins**

INGREDIENTS

- 225ml double cream
- 140ml milk
- 4 tbsp maple syrup
- 80g chopped walnuts, for mix-in

DIRECTIONS

1. In a bowl, add all ingredients (except walnuts) whisk **until smooth**.
2. Pour mixture into an empty tub, ensuring it does not go over the max fill line. Place lid on tub and freeze for 24 hours.
3. After 24 hours, remove the tub from the freezer and remove lid from tub, and let it thaw for 5 minutes. Place the tub in the Creami and lock the lid. Select ICE CREAM.
4. Twist the lid off of the outer bowl and remove the tub.
5. With a spoon, create a 4cm wide hole that reaches the bottom of the tub. Add the walnuts to the hole and process again using the MIX-IN program.
6. Once the process is finished, ice cream is ready to enjoy.

PISTACHIO ICE CREAM

Serving size 4   **Prep time 10 mins**

INGREDIENTS

- 125g pistachios
- 230ml double cream
- 180ml milk
- 70g caster sugar
- 4 egg yolks
- 65g chopped and toasted pistachios, for mix-in

DIRECTIONS

1. In a food processor, pulse the pistachios until finely ground.
2. In a saucepan, add milk, cream, sugar, egg yolk and whisk until combined.
3. Place the saucepan on hop over medium heat. Heat the mixture, stirring occasionally, until it reaches a 74-79°C. Remove from heat.
4. Strain mixture through a fine-mesh sieve into an empty tub, ensuring it does not go over the max fill line. Place tub into an ice bath. Once cooled, add the ground pistachios and stir, place lid on tub and freeze for at least 24 hours.
5. After 24 hours, remove the tub from the freezer and remove lid from tub, and let it thaw for 5 minutes. Place the tub in the Creami and lock the lid. Select GELATO.
6. Twist the lid off of the outer bowl and remove the tub.
7. With a spoon, create a 4cm wide hole that reaches the bottom of the tub. Add the chopped pistachios to the hole and process again using the MIX-IN program.
8. Once processing is complete, remove gelato from tub and serve immediately.

CARAMEL POP CORN ICE CREAM

Serving size 4   **Prep time 15 mins**

INGREDIENTS

- 225ml double cream
- 140ml milk
- 5 tbsp caramel sauce
- 30g caramel pop corn, for mix-in

DIRECTIONS

1. In a bowl, add all ingredients (except pop corn) whisk until smooth.
2. Pour mixture into an empty tub, ensuring it does not go over the max fill line. Place lid on tub and freeze for 24 hours.
3. After 24 hours, remove the tub from the freezer and remove lid from tub, and let it thaw for 5 minutes. Place the tub in the Creami and lock the lid. Select ICE CREAM.
4. Twist the lid off of the outer bowl and remove the tub.
5. With a spoon, create a 4cm wide hole that reaches the bottom of the tub. Add the pop corn to the hole and process again using the MIX-IN program.
6. Once the process is finished, ice cream is ready to enjoy.

MINT OREO ICE CREAM

Serving size 4   **Prep time 3 mins**

INGREDIENTS

- 20g cream cheese, softened
- 60g sugar
- 1 teaspoon vanilla extract
- 150ml double cream
- 230ml milk
- pinch of salt
- 3 tsp chopped fresh mint
- 2 drops of green food coloring
- 3 Oreo, broken up, for mix-in

DIRECTIONS

1. In a bowl, add all ingredients (except Oreo) and mix until combined.
2. Pour base into an empty tub, ensuring it does not go over the max fill line. Place lid on tub and freeze for 24 hours.
3. After 24 hours, remove the tub from the freezer and remove lid from tub, and let it thaw for 5 minutes. Place the tub in the Creami and lock the lid. Select ICE CREAM.
4. Twist the lid off of the outer bowl and remove the tub.
5. With a spoon, create a 4cm wide hole that reaches the bottom of the tub. Add the Oreo to the hole and process again using the MIX-IN program.
6. Once processing is complete, remove ice cream from tub and serve immediately.

DOUBLE ESPRESSO ICE CREAM

Serving size 4   **Prep time 5 mins**

INGREDIENTS

- 230ml double cream
- 150ml milk
- 4 tbsp sweetened condensed milk
- 2 tbsp espresso powder
- 2 tsp vanilla extract
- 1 pinch salt
- 50g chocolate-covered espresso beans, for mix-in

DIRECTIONS

1. In a bowl, add all ingredients (except espresso beans) whisk until smooth.
2. Pour mixture into an empty tub, ensuring it does not go over the max fill line. Place lid on tub and freeze for 24 hours.
3. After 24 hours, remove the tub from the freezer and remove lid from tub, and let it thaw for 5 minutes. Place the tub in the Creami and lock the lid. Select ICE CREAM.
4. Twist the lid off of the outer bowl and remove the tub.
5. With a spoon, create a 4cm wide hole that reaches the bottom of the tub. Add the espresso beans to the hole and process again using the MIX-IN program.
6. Once the process is finished, ice cream is ready to enjoy.

CARROT CAKE FROZEN YOGURT

Serving size 4   **Prep time 8 mins**

INGREDIENTS

- 90ml yogurt
- 135ml double cream
- 135ml milk
- 70g caster sugar
- 1 tsp ground cinnamon
- ½ tsp ground ginger
- ¼ tsp ground nutmeg
- 1 tsp vanilla extract
- 120g fresh grated carrots
- 50g chopped walnuts, for mix-in

DIRECTIONS

1. In a blender, add all ingredients (except walnuts). Blend until smooth.
2. Pour base into an empty tub, ensuring it does not go over the max fill line. Place lid on tub and freeze for 24 hours.
3. After 24 hours, remove the tub from the freezer and remove lid from tub, and let it thaw for 5 minutes. Place the tub in the Creami and lock the lid. Select ICE CREAM.
4. Twist the lid off of the outer bowl and remove the tub.
5. With a spoon, create a 4cm wide hole that reaches the bottom of the tub. Add the walnuts to the hole and process again using the MIX-IN program.
6. Once the process is finished, frozen yogurt is ready to enjoy.

SULTANA FROZEN CUSTARD

Serving size 4   **Prep time** 15 mins

INGREDIENTS

- 230ml double cream
- 180ml milk
- 4 egg yolks
- 1 tbsp caster sugar
- 1 tsp vanilla extract
- 80g Sultanas
- 50g frozen sultanas, for mix-in

DIRECTIONS

1. In a saucepan, add milk, cream, vanilla, sugar, egg yolk and whisk until combined.
2. Place the saucepan on hop over medium heat. Heat the mixture, stirring occasionally, until it reaches a 74-79°C. Remove from heat.
3. Strain mixture through a fine-mesh sieve into an empty tub, ensuring it does not go over the max fill line, add the 80g raisins. Place tub into an ice bath. Once cooled, place lid on tub and freeze for at least 24 hours.
4. After 24 hours, remove the tub from the freezer and remove lid from tub, and let it thaw for 5 minutes. Place the tub in the Creami and lock the lid. Select GELATO.
5. Twist the lid off of the outer bowl and remove the tub.
6. With a spoon, create a 4cm wide hole that reaches the bottom of the tub. Add frozen sultanas to the hole and process again using the MIX-IN program.
7. Once processing is complete, remove ice cream from tub and serve immediately.

BEE STING GELATO

Serving size 4   **Prep time** 15 mins

INGREDIENTS

- 230ml double cream
- 180ml milk
- 4 egg yolks
- 80g honey
- 1 tsp vanilla extract
- 1 tsp almond extract
- 30g chopped almonds, for mix-in
- 30g crumbled butter cookies, for mix-in

DIRECTIONS

1. In a saucepan, add milk, vanilla, almond extract, cream, sugar, egg yolk and whisk until combined.
2. Place the saucepan on hop over medium heat. Heat the mixture, stirring occasionally, until it reaches a 74-79°C. Remove from heat.
3. Strain mixture through a fine-mesh sieve into an empty tub, ensuring it does not go over the max fill line. Place tub into an ice bath. Once cooled, place lid on tub and freeze for at least 24 hours.
4. After 24 hours, remove the tub from the freezer and remove lid from tub, and let it thaw for 5 minutes. Place the tub in the Creami and lock the lid. Select GELATO.
5. Twist the lid off of the outer bowl and remove the tub.
6. With a spoon, create a 4cm wide hole that reaches the bottom of the tub. Add almonds and cookies to the hole and process again using the MIX-IN program.
7. Once processing is complete, remove ice cream from tub and serve immediately.

BLACK FOREST ICE CREAM

Serving size 4   **Prep time 5 mins**

INGREDIENTS

- 20g cream cheese, softened
- 20g cocoa powder
- 55g sugar
- 1 tsp vanilla extract
- 150ml double cream
- 230ml milk
- 50g glace cherries, for mix-in
- 20g chocolate chips, white or dark, for mix-in

DIRECTIONS

1. In a bowl, add all ingredients (except cherries and chocolate chips) whisk until smooth.
2. Pour mixture into an empty tub, ensuring it does not go over the max fill line. Place lid on tub and freeze for 24 hours.
3. After 24 hours, remove the tub from the freezer and remove lid from tub, and let it thaw for 5 minutes. Place the tub in the Creami and lock the lid. Select ICE CREAM.
4. Twist the lid off of the outer bowl and remove the tub.
5. With a spoon, create a 4cm wide hole that reaches the bottom of the tub. Add the cherries and chocolate chips to the hole and process again using the MIX-IN program.
6. Once the process is finished, ice cream is ready to enjoy.

COFFEE TOFFEE ICE CREAM

Serving size 4   **Prep time 5 mins**

INGREDIENTS

- 120ml milk
- 240ml double cream
- 70g sugar
- Pinch of salt
- 2 tbsp Instant Coffee
- 70g chopped toffee candy, for mix-in

DIRECTIONS

1. In a bowl, add all ingredients (except toffee candy) and mix until combined.
2. Pour base into an empty tub, ensuring it does not go over the max fill line. Place lid on tub and freeze for 24 hours.
3. After 24 hours, remove the tub from the freezer and remove lid from tub, and let it thaw for 5 minutes. Place the tub in the Creami and lock the lid. Select ICE CREAM.
4. Twist the lid off of the outer bowl and remove the tub.
5. With a spoon, create a 4cm wide hole that reaches the bottom of the tub. Add the toffee candy to the hole and process again using the MIX-IN program.
6. Once processing is complete, remove ice cream from tub and serve immediately.

CHOCOLATE BROWNIE ICE CREAM

Serving size 4   **Prep time 4 mins**

INGREDIENTS

- 140ml milk
- 250ml double cream
- 70g sugar
- Pinch of salt
- 30g cocoa powder
- 50g brownies, for mix-in

DIRECTIONS

1. In a bowl, add all ingredients (except brownies) and mix until combined.
2. Pour base into an empty tub, ensuring it does not go over the max fill line. Place lid on tub and freeze for 24 hours.
3. After 24 hours, remove the tub from the freezer and remove lid from tub, and let it thaw for 5 minutes. Place the tub in the Creami and lock the lid. Select ICE CREAM.
4. Twist the lid off of the outer bowl and remove the tub.
5. With a spoon, create a 4cm wide hole that reaches the bottom of the tub. Add the brownies to the hole and process again using the MIX-IN program.
6. Once processing is complete, remove ice cream from tub and garnish with additional brownie chunks serve immediately.

COFFEE AND WALNUT ICE CREAM

Serving size 4   **Prep time 4 mins**

INGREDIENTS

- 150ml milk
- 250ml double cream
- 70g sugar
- Pinch of salt
- 30g cocoa powder
- 1 tsp instant coffee
- 50g chopped walnuts, for mix-in

DIRECTIONS

1. In a bowl, add all ingredients (except walnuts) and mix until combined.
2. Pour base into an empty tub, ensuring it does not go over the max fill line. Place lid on tub and freeze for 24 hours.
3. After 24 hours, remove the tub from the freezer and remove lid from tub, and let it thaw for 5 minutes. Place the tub in the Creami and lock the lid. Select ICE CREAM.
4. Twist the lid off of the outer bowl and remove the tub.
5. With a spoon, create a 4cm wide hole that reaches the bottom of the tub. Add the walnuts to the hole and process again using the MIX-IN program.
6. Once processing is complete, remove ice cream from tub and serve immediately.

CHOCOLATE MOCHA GELATO

Serving size 4   **Prep time 15 mins**

INGREDIENTS

- 230ml double cream
- 180ml milk
- 4 egg yolks
- 1 tbsp espresso powder
- 2 tbsp cocoa powder
- 40g caster sugar

DIRECTIONS

1. In a saucepan, add milk, espresso powder, cocoa powder, **cream, sugar, egg yolk and** whisk until combined.
2. Place the saucepan on hop over medium heat. Heat the mixture, stirring occasionally, until it reaches a 74-79°C. Remove from heat.
3. Strain mixture through a fine-mesh sieve into an empty tub, ensuring it does not go over the max fill line. Place tub into an ice bath. Once cooled, place lid on tub and freeze for at least 24 hours.
4. After 24 hours, remove the tub from the freezer and remove lid from tub, and let it thaw for 5 minutes. Place the tub in the Creami and lock the lid. **Select GELATO.**
5. Once processing is complete, remove gelato from tub and **serve immediately.**

RICOTTA ICE CREAM

Serving size 4   **Prep time 4 mins**

INGREDIENTS

- 200g Ricotta, at room temperature
- 100g sugar
- 150ml Milk
- 50g cookies of your choice, for mix-in

DIRECTIONS

1. In a blender, add all ingredients (except cookies). Blend until **smooth.**
2. Pour base into an empty tub, ensuring it does not go over the max fill line. Place lid on tub and freeze for 24 hours.
3. After 24 hours, remove the tub from the freezer and remove lid from tub, and let it thaw for 5 minutes. Place the tub in the Creami and lock the lid. Select ICE CREAM.
4. Twist the lid off of the outer bowl and remove the tub.
5. With a spoon, create a 4cm wide hole that reaches the bottom of the tub. Add the cookies to the hole and process again using the MIX-IN program.
6. Once the process is finished, ice cream is ready to enjoy.

RASPBERRY WHITE CHOCOLATE GELATO

Serving size 4   **Prep time** 15 mins

INGREDIENTS

- 230ml double cream
- 180ml milk
- 4 egg yolks
- 40g caster sugar
- 100g White Chocolate, melted
- 50g frozen raspberries
- 1 tsp vanilla extract

DIRECTIONS

1. In a saucepan, add milk, chocolate, cream, sugar, egg yolk and whisk until combined.
2. Place the saucepan on hop over medium heat. Heat the mixture, stirring occasionally, until it reaches a 74-79°C. Remove from heat.
3. Strain mixture through a fine-mesh sieve into an empty tub, ensuring it does not go over the max fill line. Place tub into an ice bath. Once cooled, place lid on tub and freeze for at least 24 hours.
4. After 24 hours, remove the tub from the freezer and remove lid from tub, and let it thaw for 5 minutes. Place the tub in the Creami and lock the lid. Select GELATO.
5. Twist the lid off of the outer bowl and remove the tub.
6. With a spoon, create a 4cm wide hole that reaches the bottom of the tub. Add raspberries to the hole and process again using the MIX-IN program.
7. Once processing is complete, remove ice cream from tub and serve immediately.

CHERRY VANILLA FROZEN YOGURT

Serving size 4   **Prep time** 3 mins

INGREDIENTS

- 90ml plain yogurt
- 135ml double cream
- 135ml milk
- 70g sugar
- 1 tsp vanilla extract
- 50g frozen cherries, for mix-in

DIRECTIONS

1. In a blender, add all ingredients (except cherries). Blend until smooth.
2. Pour base into an empty tub, ensuring it does not go over the max fill line. Place lid on tub and freeze for 24 hours.
3. After 24 hours, remove the tub from the freezer and remove lid from tub, and let it thaw for 5 minutes. Place the tub in the Creami and lock the lid. Select ICE CREAM.
4. Twist the lid off of the outer bowl and remove the tub.
5. With a spoon, create a 4cm wide hole that reaches the bottom of the tub. Add the cherries to the hole and process again using the MIX-IN program.
6. Once the process is finished, ice cream is ready to enjoy.

GINGERBREAD ICE CREAM

Serving size 4   **Prep time 6 mins**

INGREDIENTS

- 230ml milk
- 150ml double cream
- 70g brown sugar
- 30g cream cheese
- 1/2 tsp ground ginger
- 1/2 tsp ground cinnamon
- Pinch of nutmeg
- Pinch of ground cloves
- 60g gingerbread cookies, for mix-in

DIRECTIONS

1. In a bowl, add all ingredients (except gingerbread cookies) and mix until combined.
2. Pour base into an empty tub, ensuring it does not go over the max fill line. Place lid on tub and freeze for 24 hours.
3. After 24 hours, remove the tub from the freezer and remove lid from tub, and let it thaw for 5 minutes. Place the tub in the Creami and lock the lid. Select ICE CREAM.
4. Twist the lid off of the outer bowl and remove the tub.
5. With a spoon, create a 4cm wide hole that reaches the bottom of the tub. Add the gingerbread cookies to the hole and process again using the MIX-IN program.
6. Once processing is complete, remove ice cream from tub and serve immediately.

CARAMEL BANANA ICE CREAM

Serving size 4   **Prep time 4 mins**

INGREDIENTS

- 18g cream cheese, softened
- 1 large ripe banana, sliced
- 50g caramel sauce/syrup
- 150ml double cream
- 250ml milk

DIRECTIONS

1. In a bowl, add all ingredients (except banana) whisk until smooth.
2. Pour mixture into an empty tub, ensuring it does not go over the max fill line, add the banana. Place lid on tub and freeze for 24 hours.
3. After 24 hours, remove the tub from the freezer and remove lid from tub, and let it thaw for 5 minutes. Place the tub in the Creami and lock the lid. Select ICE CREAM.
4. Once the process is finished, serve the ice cream scoops in bowls or cones, and drizzle extra caramel sauce on top.

HONEY LAVENDER ICE CREAM

Serving size 4   **Prep time 5 mins**

INGREDIENTS

- 18g cream cheese, softened
- 50g honey
- 3 tbsp dried culinary lavender
- 150ml double cream
- 230ml milk

DIRECTIONS

1. In a bowl, add all ingredients whisk until smooth.
2. Pour mixture into an empty tub, ensuring it does not go **over the max fill line**. Place lid on tub and freeze for 24 hours.
3. After 24 hours, remove the tub from the freezer and remove lid from tub, and let it thaw for 5 minutes. Place the tub in the Creami and lock the lid. Select ICE CREAM.
4. Once the process is finished, ice cream is ready to enjoy.

PEACH CRUMBLE ICE CREAM

Serving size 4   **Prep time 5 mins**

INGREDIENTS

- 225g ripe or tinned peaches, peeled and diced
- 250ml double cream
- 80g sugar
- 1 tsp vanilla extract
- 1/4 tsp cinnamon
- 70g crushed cookies, for mix-in

DIRECTIONS

1. In a bowl, add all ingredients (except cookies) whisk until smooth.
2. Pour mixture into an empty tub, ensuring it does not go over the max fill line. Place lid on tub and freeze for 24 hours.
3. After 24 hours, remove the tub from the freezer and remove lid from tub, and let it thaw for 5 minutes. Place the tub in the Creami and lock the lid. Select ICE CREAM.
4. Twist the lid off of the outer bowl and remove the tub.
5. With a spoon, create a 4cm wide hole that reaches the bottom of the tub. Add the cookies to the hole and process again using the MIX-IN program.
6. Once the process is finished, ice cream is ready to enjoy.

COCONUT AVOCADO ICE CREAM

Serving size 4   **Prep time** 10 mins

INGREDIENTS

- 18g cream cheese, softened
- 1 ripe avocado, peeled and pitted
- 150ml double cream
- 250ml coconut milk

DIRECTIONS

1. In a bowl, add all ingredients (except avocado) whisk until smooth.
2. Pour mixture into an empty tub, ensuring it does not go over the max fill line, add the avocado. Place lid on tub and freeze for 24 hours.
3. After 24 hours, remove the tub from the freezer and remove lid from tub, and let it thaw for 5 minutes. Place the tub in the Creami and lock the lid. Select ICE CREAM.
4. Once the process is finished, scoop into bowls or cones and serve.

CINNAMON APPLE ICE CREAM

Serving size 4   **Prep time** 15 mins

INGREDIENTS

- 20g cream cheese, softened
- 70g brown sugar
- 1 tsp cinnamon
- 150ml double cream
- 230ml milk
- 1 tbsp butter
- 250g apples, peeled and diced

DIRECTIONS

1. In a saucepan, melt the butter over medium heat. Add the apples, brown sugar, and cinnamon. Cook until the apples are soft and caramelised, about 8-10 minutes. Remove from heat, transfer to a bowl and let it cool completely.
2. once cooled, add cream and milk and mix until combined.
3. Pour base into an empty tub, ensuring it does not go over the max fill line. Place lid on tub and freeze for 24 hours.
4. After 24 hours, remove the tub from the freezer and remove lid from tub, and let it thaw for 5 minutes. Place the tub in the Creami and lock the lid. Select ICE CREAM.
5. Once processing is complete, remove ice cream from tub and serve immediately.

CHELSEA BUNS ICE CREAM

Serving size 4   **Prep time 5 mins**

INGREDIENTS

- 20g cream cheese, softened
- 80g condensed milk
- 200ml double cream
- ½ tsp vanilla extract
- 1 tsp ground cinnamon
- 60g crushed Biscoff, for mix-in

DIRECTIONS

1. In a bowl, add all ingredients (except speculoos) and mix until combined.
2. Pour base into an empty tub, ensuring it does not go over the max fill line. Place lid on tub and freeze for 24 hours.
3. After 24 hours, remove the tub from the freezer and remove lid from tub, and let it thaw for 5 minutes. Place the tub in the Creami and lock the lid. Select ICE CREAM.
4. Twist the lid off of the outer bowl and remove the tub.
5. With a spoon, create a 4cm wide hole that reaches the bottom of the tub. Add the Biscoff to the and process again using the MIX-IN program.
6. Once processing is complete, remove ice cream from tub and serve immediately.

BIRTHDAY CAKE ICE CREAM

Serving size 4   **Prep time 4 mins**

INGREDIENTS

- 20g cream cheese, softened
- 80g condensed milk
- 200ml double cream
- 1/4 tsp salt
- 1/4 tsp almond extract
- 1/4 tsp vanilla extract
- 20g sprinkles, for mix-in
- 1 vanilla cupcake broken into large chunks, for mix-in

DIRECTIONS

1. In a bowl, add all ingredients (except cupcake) and mix until combined.
2. Pour base into an empty tub, ensuring it does not go over the max fill line. Place lid on tub and freeze for 24 hours.
3. After 24 hours, remove the tub from the freezer and remove lid from tub, and let it thaw for 5 minutes. Place the tub in the Creami and lock the lid. Select ICE CREAM.
4. Twist the lid off of the outer bowl and remove the tub.
5. With a spoon, create a 4cm wide hole that reaches the bottom of the tub. Add the cupcake to the hole and process again using the MIX-IN program.
6. Once processing is complete, remove ice cream from tub and serve immediately.

PINEAPPLE GINGER FROZEN YOGURT

Serving size 4   **Prep time 5 mins**

INGREDIENTS

- 90ml plain whole milk yogurt
- 135ml double cream
- 135ml whole milk
- 70g caster sugar
- 1 tsp grated fresh ginger
- 1 tsp vanilla extract
- 150g fresh or canned pineapple, chopped

DIRECTIONS

1. In a bowl, add all ingredients and mix until combined.
2. Pour base into an empty tub, ensuring it does not go over the max fill line. Place lid on tub and freeze for 24 hours.
3. After 24 hours, remove the tub from the freezer and remove lid from tub, and let it thaw for 5 minutes. Place the tub in the Creami and lock the lid. Select ICE CREAM.
4. Once processing is complete, remove frozen yogurt from tub and serve immediately.

MATCHA GREEN TEA FROZEN YOGURT

Serving size 4   **Prep time 5 mins**

INGREDIENTS

- 90ml plain yogurt
- 135ml double cream
- 135ml whole milk
- 70g caster sugar
- 1 tsp matcha powder
- 50g chocolate chips, for mix-in

DIRECTIONS

1. In a bowl, add all ingredients (except chocolate chips) and mix until combined.
2. Pour base into an empty tub, ensuring it does not go over the max fill line. Place lid on tub and freeze for 24 hours.
3. After 24 hours, remove the tub from the freezer and remove lid from tub, and let it thaw for 5 minutes. Place the tub in the Creami and lock the lid. Select ICE CREAM.
4. Twist the lid off of the outer bowl and remove the tub.
5. With a spoon, create a 4cm wide hole that reaches the bottom of the tub. Add the chocolate chips to the hole and process again using the MIX-IN program.
6. Once processing is complete, remove frozen yogurt from tub and serve immediately.

EARL GREY GELATO

Serving size 4   **Prep time 26 mins**

INGREDIENTS

- 230ml double cream
- 180ml milk
- 4 egg yolks
- 40g caster sugar
- 3 Earl Grey tea bags

DIRECTIONS

1. In a saucepan, add milk, sugar, cream, egg yolk and whisk until combined.
2. Place the saucepan on hop over medium heat. Heat the mixture, stirring occasionally, until it reaches a 74-79°C. Remove from heat. Add the Earl Grey tea bags to the cream mixture. Cover the saucepan and let the tea steep in the cream for about 15 minutes.
3. Strain mixture through a fine-mesh sieve into an empty tub, ensuring it does not go over the max fill line. Place tub into an ice bath. Once cooled, place lid on tub and freeze for at least 24 hours.
4. After 24 hours, remove the tub from the freezer and remove lid from tub, and let it thaw for 5 minutes. Place the tub in the Creami and lock the lid. Select GELATO.
5. Once processing is complete, remove the gelato from tub and serve immediately.

You can use any tea flavour you like

DATE ICE CREAM

Serving size 4   **Prep time 4 mins**

INGREDIENTS

- 20g cream cheese, softened
- 20g brown sugar
- 1 tsp vanilla extract
- 150ml double cream
- 230ml whole milk
- 120g dates, pitted and chopped

DIRECTIONS

1. In a bowl, add all ingredients (except dates) whisk until smooth.
2. Pour mixture into an empty tub, ensuring it does not go over the max fill line. Add the dates and place lid on tub and freeze for 24 hours.
3. After 24 hours, remove the tub from the freezer and remove lid from tub, and let it thaw for 5 minutes. Place the tub in the Creami and lock the lid. Select ICE CREAM.
4. Once the process is finished, ice cream is ready to enjoy.

39

POPPY SEED ICE CREAM

Serving size 4   **Prep time 4 mins**

INGREDIENTS

- 150ml milk
- 250ml double cream
- 80g poppy seeds
- 1 1/2 tsp almond extract
- 100g sugar
- 1/2 tsp vanilla extract

DIRECTIONS

1. In a bowl, add all ingredients whisk until smooth.
2. Pour mixture into an empty tub, ensuring it does not go over the max fill line. Place lid on tub and freeze for 24 hours.
3. After 24 hours, remove the tub from the freezer and remove lid from tub, and let it thaw for 5 minutes. Place the tub in the Creami and lock the lid. Select ICE CREAM.
4. Once the process is finished, ice cream is ready to enjoy.

SALTED CARAMEL PRETZEL ICE CREAM

Serving size 4   **Prep time 5 mins**

INGREDIENTS

- 18g cream cheese, softened
- 55g sugar
- 3 tbsp salted caramel sauce
- 150ml double cream
- 230ml milk
- 70g chopped pretzels, for mix

DIRECTIONS

1. In a bowl, add all ingredients (except pretzels) whisk until smooth.
2. Pour mixture into an empty tub, ensuring it does not go over the max fill line. Place lid on tub and freeze for 24 hours.
3. After 24 hours, remove the tub from the freezer and remove lid from tub, and let it thaw for 5 minutes. Place the tub in the Creami and lock the lid. Select ICE CREAM.
4. Twist the lid off of the outer bowl and remove the tub.
5. With a spoon, create a 4cm wide hole that reaches the bottom of the tub. Add the pretzels to the hole and process again using the MIX-IN program.
6. Once the process is finished, ice cream is ready to enjoy.

PEAR HELENE ICE CREAM

Serving size **4**   Prep time **5 mins**

INGREDIENTS

- 250g canned pears, drained
- 50g sugar
- 1 tsp vanilla extract
- 1 tsp lemon juice
- 250ml double cream
- 50g chopped chocolate, for mix-in
- 20g sliced almonds, toasted, for mix-in

DIRECTIONS

1. In a bowl, add all ingredients (except pears and mix-ins) whisk until smooth.
2. Pour mixture into an empty tub, ensuring it does not go over the max fill line, add the pears. Place lid on tub and freeze for 24 hours.
3. After 24 hours, remove the tub from the freezer and remove lid from tub, and let it thaw for 5 minutes. Place the tub in the Creami and lock the lid. Select ICE CREAM.
4. Twist the lid off of the outer bowl and remove the tub.
5. With a spoon, create a 4cm wide hole that reaches the bottom of the tub. Add the chocolate and almonds to the hole and process again using the MIX-IN program.
6. Once the process is finished, ice cream is ready to enjoy.

RHUBARB COMPOTE ICE CREAM

Serving size **4**   Prep time **3 mins**

INGREDIENTS

- 200g Rhubarb Compote
- 40g sugar
- 1 tsp lemon juice
- 250ml double cream

DIRECTIONS

1. In a bowl, add all ingredients (except Rhubarb). Whisk until combined.
2. Pour mixture into Ninja Creami tub container, ensuring it does not go over the max fill line. Add the Rhubarb. Freeze the tub for 24 hours.
3. After 24 hours, remove the tub from the freezer, and plug in your Ninja Creami.
4. Remove the lid from the tub and grab Ninja Creami outer bowl. Place tub securely into the outer bowl and cover with lid. Once lid is on, place the outer bowl into the machine, twisting to the right until it locks into place. Press the "Ice Cream" button
5. Once processing is complete, remove yogurt from tub and serve immediately.

PEPPERMINT CANDY CANE ICE CREAM

Serving size 4   **Prep time 3 mins**

INGREDIENTS

- 240ml double cream
- 150ml milk
- 60g sugar
- 1 1/2 tsp peppermint extract
- pinch of salt
- 3 drops red food coloring
- 4 medium candy canes crushed, for mix-in

DIRECTIONS

1. In a bowl, add all ingredients (except candy canes) and mix until combined.
2. Pour base into an empty tub, ensuring it does **not go over the max fill line. Place** lid on tub and freeze for 24 hours.
3. After 24 hours, remove the tub from the freezer **and remove lid from tub, and let it thaw** for 5 minutes. Place the tub in the Creami and **lock the lid. Select ICE CREAM.**
4. Twist the lid off of the outer bowl and remove **the tub.**
5. With a spoon, create a 4cm wide hole that reaches the bottom of the tub. Add the candy canes to the HOLE and process again using the MIX-IN program.
6. Once processing is complete, remove ice cream from tub and serve immediately.

SPICED PLUM FROZEN YOGURT

Serving size 4   **Prep time 3 mins**

INGREDIENTS

- 90ml yogurt
- 135ml double cream
- 135ml milk
- 70g sugar
- 120g ripe plums, pitted and diced
- 1 tsp cinnamon
- Pinch of nutmeg

DIRECTIONS

1. In a bowl, add all ingredients and mix until combined.
2. Pour base into an empty tub, ensuring it does not go over the max fill line. Place lid on tub and freeze for 24 hours.
3. After 24 hours, remove the tub from the freezer and remove lid from tub, and let it thaw for 5 minutes. Place the tub in the Creami and lock the lid. Select ICE CREAM.
4. Once processing is complete, remove frozen yogurt from tub and serve immediately.

Smoothie Bowl

POMEGRANATE SMOOTHIE BOWL

Serving size: **4**   **Prep time:** **5 mins**

INGREDIENTS

- 150g frozen berries
- 1 large ripe banana, sliced
- 80g fresh pomegranate seeds
- 150ml yogurt
- 100ml milk
- ½ tsp vanilla extract

Toppings :
- Dried coconut, granola, fresh berries, fresh pomegranate seeds.

DIRECTIONS

1. Fill an empty tub with fruit in order of ingredients. Add the vanilla extract.
2. Cover fruit with yogurt and milk. Place lid on tub and freeze for 24 hours.
3. After 24 hours, remove the tub from the freezer and remove lid from tub, and let it thaw for 5 minutes. Place the tub in the Creami and lock the lid. Select SMOOTHIE BOWL.
4. Once the process is finished, Transfer into bowls and decorate with Dried coconut, granola, fresh berries, fresh pomegranate seeds. Serve.

RASPBERRY AVOCADO SMOOTHIE BOWL

Serving size 4   **Prep time 5 mins**

INGREDIENTS

- 150g raspberries, frozen or fresh
- ¼ ripe avocado, sliced
- 150ml milk
- 100ml yogurt

Toppings :
- Nuts, granola, dried berries, coconut cubes, mint leaves.

DIRECTIONS

1. Fill an empty tub with fruit in order of ingredients. Add the **vanilla extract.**
2. Cover fruit with yogurt and milk. Place lid on tub and freeze for 24 hours.
3. After 24 hours, remove the tub from the freezer and remove lid from tub, and let it thaw for 5 minutes. Place the tub in the Creami and lock the lid. Select SMOOTHIE BOWL.
4. Once the process is finished, Transfer into bowls and decorate with Nuts, granola, dried berries, coconut cubes, mint leaves. Serve.

PUMPKIN SMOOTHIE BOWL

Serving size 2   **Prep time** 5 mins

INGREDIENTS

- 225g pumpkin puree
- 1–2 dates, pitted & diced
- 1 tbsp honey
- 2 tbsp almond butter
- ½ tsp vanilla extract
- ½ tsp cinnamon
- Pinch of nutmeg
- Pinch of ginger
- 1 ripe banana, peeled
- 60ml yogurt

Toppings :
- Nuts, granola, chia seeds.

DIRECTIONS

1. Place all ingredients into empty tub in the order listed Place lid on tub and freeze for 24 hours.
2. After 24 hours, remove the tub from the freezer and remove lid from tub, and let it thaw for 5 minutes. Place the tub in the Creami and lock the lid. Select SMOOTHIE BOWL.
3. Once the process is finished, Transfer into bowls and decorate with Nuts, granola, chia seeds. Serve.

MANGO TROPICAL SMOOTHIE BOWL

Serving size 4   **Prep time** 5 mins

INGREDIENTS

- 100g ripe mango, peeled & cut into cubes
- 100g pineapple, cut into cubes
- 1 ripe banana, sliced
- Juice of 1 orange
- 100ml yogurt
- 150ml milk

Topping:
- handful blueberries
- 2 tbsp coconut flakes
- 1 tsp chia seeds

DIRECTIONS

1. Place all ingredients into empty tub in the order listed Place lid on tub and freeze for 24 hours.
2. After 24 hours, remove the tub from the freezer and remove lid from tub, and let it thaw for 5 minutes. Place the tub in the Creami and lock the lid. Select SMOOTHIE BOWL.
3. Once the process is finished, Transfer into bowls and decorate with, blueberries, coconut flakes and chia seeds. Serve.

GREEN SMOOTHIE BOWL

Serving size 4   **Prep time 5 mins**

INGREDIENTS

- 3 kiwi, peeled & sliced
- 30g baby spinach
- 200g pineapple, chopped
- 1 orange, peeled and chopped
- 1 banana, sliced
- 1 tbsp lemon juice
- 1 tbsp honey
- 150ml yogurt
- 150ml milk

Topping:
- 20g pistachio
- Shredded coconut

DIRECTIONS

1. Place all ingredients into empty tub in the order listed Place lid on tub and freeze for 24 hours.
2. After 24 hours, remove the tub from the freezer and remove lid from tub, and let it thaw for 5 minutes. Place the tub in the Creami and lock the lid. Select SMOOTHIE BOWL.
3. Once the process is finished, Transfer into bowls and Garnish with pistachio, Shredded coconut. Serve.

TURMERIC SMOOTHIE BOWL

Serving size 4   **Prep time 5 mins**

INGREDIENTS

- 4 medium bananas, peeled & sliced
- 4 tbsp lemon juice
- 1 ½ tsp ground turmeric
- 1 tsp ground ginger
- Pinch of pepper
- 150ml milk

Topping:
- Raspberries
- Blueberries
- Kiwi slices

DIRECTIONS

1. Place all ingredients into empty tub in the order listed Place lid on tub **and freeze** for 24 hours.
2. After 24 hours, remove the tub from the freezer and remove lid from tub, and let it thaw for 5 minutes. Place the tub in the Creami and lock the lid. Select SMOOTHIE BOWL.
3. Once the process is finished, Transfer into bowls and Garnish with Raspberries, Blueberries and kiwi slices. Serve.

MANGO SMOOTHIE BOWL

Serving size 4 **Prep time 5 mins**

INGREDIENTS

- 200g mangoes, peeled & chopped
- 2 tsp honey
- 1 banana, sliced
- 100ml milk
- 150ml yogurt

Topping:
- Mango cubes
- Kiwi slices

DIRECTIONS

1. Place all ingredients into empty tub in the order listed Place lid on tub and freeze for 24 hours.
2. After 24 hours, remove the tub from the freezer and remove lid from tub, and let it thaw for 5 minutes. Place the tub in the Creami and lock the lid. Select SMOOTHIE BOWL.
3. Once the process is finished, Transfer into bowls and Garnish with Mango cubes, and kiwi slices. Serve.

MATCHA SMOOTHIE BOWL

Serving size 4 **Prep time 5 mins**

INGREDIENTS

- 1 banana, peeled & sliced
- 1 tsp matcha powder
- 30g fresh baby spinach
- 1 kiwi, peeled & sliced
- 2 tsp honey
- 100ml milk

- 150ml yogurt

Topping:
- Raspberries
- Pumpkin seeds

DIRECTIONS

1. Place all ingredients into empty tub in the order listed Place lid on tub and freeze for 24 hours.
2. After 24 hours, remove the tub from the freezer and remove lid from tub, and let it thaw for 5 minutes. Place the tub in the Creami and lock the lid. Select SMOOTHIE BOWL.
3. Once the process is finished, Transfer into bowls and Garnish with Pumpkin seeds, and Raspberries. Serve.

DRAGON FRUIT SMOOTHIE BOWL

Serving size 4   **Prep time** 5 mins

INGREDIENTS

- 200g dragon fruit, chopped
- 90g raspberries
- 1 tbsp honey
- 1 ripe banana, sliced
- 100ml milk
- 150ml yogurt

Topping:
- Banana slices
- Nuts
- Shredded coconut

DIRECTIONS

1. Place all ingredients into empty tub in the order listed Place lid on tub and freeze for 24 hours.
2. After 24 hours, remove the tub from the freezer and remove lid from tub, and let it thaw for 5 minutes. Place the tub in the Creami and lock the lid. Select SMOOTHIE BOWL.
3. Once the process is finished, Transfer into bowls and Garnish with Banana slices, Nuts and Shredded coconut. Serve.

RASPBERRY PEACH SMOOTHIE BOWL

Serving size 4   **Prep time** 5 mins

INGREDIENTS

- 150g raspberries
- 150g canned peaches
- 100ml milk
- 150ml yogurt

Topping:
- Nuts
- Raspberries

DIRECTIONS

1. Place all ingredients into empty tub in the order listed Place lid on tub and freeze for 24 hours.
2. After 24 hours, remove the tub from the freezer and remove lid from tub, and let it thaw for 5 minutes. Place the tub in the Creami and lock the lid. Select SMOOTHIE BOWL.
3. Once the process is finished, Transfer into bowls and garnish with nuts and raspberries. Serve.

PEACH PIE SMOOTHIE BOWL

Serving size 4   **Prep time** 5 mins

INGREDIENTS

- 200g peaches, sliced
- 1 tbsp almond butter
- 1 tbsp honey
- 1/2 tsp cinnamon
- 1/2 tsp vanilla extract
- pinch of nutmeg
- 100ml milk
- 150ml yogurt

Topping:
- peach slices
- Nuts
- Berries

DIRECTIONS

1. Place all ingredients into empty tub in the order listed Place lid on tub and freeze for 24 hours.
2. After 24 hours, remove the tub from the freezer and remove lid from tub, and let it thaw for 5 minutes. Place the tub in the Creami and lock the lid. Select SMOOTHIE BOWL.
3. Once the process is finished, Transfer into bowls and Garnish with peach slices, Nuts and berries. Serve.

BLUEBERRY BANANA SMOOTHIE BOWL

Serving size 4   **Prep time** 5 mins

INGREDIENTS

- 3 bananas, sliced
- 150g blueberries
- 2 tbsp chia seeds
- ½ tsp vanilla extract
- 100ml milk
- 150ml yogurt

Topping:
- Banana slices
- Berries
- Granola

DIRECTIONS

1. Place all ingredients into empty tub in the order listed Place lid on tub and freeze for 24 hours.
2. After 24 hours, remove the tub from the freezer and remove lid from tub, and let it thaw for 5 minutes. Place the tub in the Creami and lock the lid. Select SMOOTHIE BOWL.
3. Once the process is finished, Transfer into bowls and Garnish with banana slices, granola and berries. Serve.

LIME COCONUT SMOOTHIE BOWL

Serving size 4   **Prep time** 5 mins

INGREDIENTS

- 1 banana, sliced
- 30g fresh baby spinach
- 100g pineapple, chopped
- 100g mango, chopped
- 20g shredded coconut
- 3 tbsp honey
- 2 tsp lime zest
- 1 tsp lime juice
- 1/2 tsp vanilla extract
- 100ml coconut milk
- 150ml yogurt

Topping:
- Raspberries

DIRECTIONS

1. Place all ingredients into empty tub in the order listed Place lid on tub and freeze for 24 hours.
2. After 24 hours, remove the tub from the freezer and remove lid from tub, and let it thaw for 5 minutes. Place the tub in the Creami and lock the lid. Select SMOOTHIE BOWL.
3. Once the process is finished, Transfer into bowls and Garnish with raspberries. Serve.

PEANUT BUTTER SMOOTHIE BOWL

Serving size 4   **Prep time** 5 mins

INGREDIENTS

- 1 large banana, peeled
- 1 tsp cocoa powder
- 1 tbsp ground flaxseed
- 60g peanut butter
- 1 tbsp honey
- 100ml milk
- 150ml yogurt

Topping:
- Granola

DIRECTIONS

1. Place all ingredients into empty tub in the order listed. Place lid on tub and freeze for 24 hours.
2. After 24 hours, remove the tub from the freezer and remove lid from tub, and let it thaw for 5 minutes. Place the tub in the Creami and lock the lid. Select SMOOTHIE BOWL.
3. Once the process is finished, Transfer into bowls and Garnish with Granola. Serve.

COFFEE SMOOTHIE BOWL

Serving size 4   **Prep time** 5 mins

INGREDIENTS

- 1 banana, sliced
- 2 tbsp cacao powder
- 120ml cold brewed coffee
- 150ml yogurt

Topping:
- Shredded coconut
- Banana slices
- Chocolate chips

DIRECTIONS

1. Place all ingredients into empty tub in the order listed. Place lid on tub and freeze for 24 hours.
2. After 24 hours, remove the tub from the freezer and remove lid from tub, and let it thaw for 5 minutes. Place the tub in the Creami and lock the lid. Select SMOOTHIE BOWL.
3. Once the process is finished, Transfer into bowls and garnish with shredded coconut and banana slices and chocolate chips. Serve.

APPLE CINNAMON SMOOTHIE BOWL

Serving size 4   **Prep time** 5 mins

INGREDIENTS

- 1 medium apple, peeled and chopped
- 1/2 tsp cinnamon
- 1 banana, sliced
- 100ml milk
- 150ml yogurt

Topping:
- Chopped almond
- Apple slices
- Banana slices

DIRECTIONS

1. Place all ingredients into empty tub in the order listed Place lid on tub and freeze for 24 hours.
2. After 24 hours, remove the tub from the freezer and remove lid from tub, and let it thaw for 5 minutes. Place the tub in the Creami and lock the lid. Select SMOOTHIE BOWL.
3. Once the process is finished, Transfer into bowls and Garnish with chia seeds and Banana slices. Serve.

Milkshake

STRAWBERRY CHEESECAKE MILKSHAKE

Serving size **4**   Prep time **2 mins**

INGREDIENTS

- 80g cream cheese, softened
- 150g vanilla ice cream
- 100ml milk
- 100g fresh strawberries, sliced

Topping:
- Biscuit/cookie crumbs
- whipped cream
- Chocolate sauce

DIRECTIONS

1. Place all ingredients into empty tub in the order listed (except toppings).
2. Place tub in outer bowl, install the Paddle onto outer bowl lid, and lock the lid assembly on the outer bowl. Place bowl assembly on motor base and twist the handle right to raise the platform and lock in place. Select MILKSHAKE.
3. Remove the milkshake from the tub and Garnish with cookie crumbs, whipped cream and chocolate sauce. Serve.

STRAWBERRY COCONUT LIME MILKSHAKE

Serving size **1-2**   Prep time **2 mins**

INGREDIENTS

- 1 tbsp lime juice
- 1 tsp honey
- 150g vanilla ice cream
- 100ml coconut milk
- 100g fresh strawberries, sliced

DIRECTIONS

1. Place all ingredients into empty tub in the order listed.
2. Place tub in outer bowl, install the Paddle onto outer bowl lid, and lock the lid assembly on the outer bowl. Place bowl assembly on motor base and twist the handle right to raise the platform and lock in place. Select MILKSHAKE.
3. Once processing is complete, remove milkshake from tub and serve immediately.

CHOCOLATE ALMOND MILKSHAKE

Serving size 1-2   **Prep time** 3 mins

INGREDIENTS

- 200g vanilla ice cream
- 100ml almond milk
- 1 tbsp almond butter
- 80ml chocolate syrup

Topping:
- Whipped cream
- Chopped almonds
- Chocolate sauce

DIRECTIONS

1. Place all ingredients into empty tub in the order listed.
2. Place tub in outer bowl, install the Paddle onto outer bowl lid, and lock the lid assembly on the outer bowl. Place bowl assembly on motor base and twist the handle right to raise the platform and lock in place. Select MILKSHAKE.
3. Remove the milkshake from the tub and top with chopped almonds, chocolate sauce and chocolate chips. serve.

SALTED CARAMEL BISCOFF MILKSHAKE

Serving size 1-2   **Prep time** 3 mins

INGREDIENTS

- 100ml milk
- 200g vanilla ice cream
- 2 tbsp Biscoff cookie butter
- 1/2 tsp cinnamon
- A pinch of sea salt

Topping:
- Biscoff cookie, crumbled
- Biscoff cookie butter
- Caramel sauce
- sea salt

DIRECTIONS

1. Place all ingredients into empty tub in the order listed.
2. Place tub in outer bowl, install the Paddle onto outer bowl lid, and lock the lid assembly on the outer bowl. Place bowl assembly on motor base and twist the handle right to raise the platform and lock in place. Select MILKSHAKE.
3. Remove the milkshake from the tub, spread few tablespoons of Biscoff cookie butter around the top edge of the milkshake glasses, drizzle caramel sauce and a sprinkle of flaked sea salt add milkshake. serve.

CHOCOLATE CHIP COOKIE MILKSHAKE

Serving size 1-2 **Prep time 3 mins**

INGREDIENTS

- 6 Chocolate Chip cookies
- 1 tsp cocoa powder
- 100ml milk
- 200g vanilla ice cream

Topping:
- Crushed cookies

DIRECTIONS

1. Place all ingredients into empty tub in the order listed, (no need to make a hole)
2. Place tub in outer bowl, install the Paddle onto outer bowl lid, and lock the lid assembly on the outer bowl. Place bowl assembly on motor base and twist the handle right to raise the platform and lock in place. Select MILKSHAKE.
3. Remove the milkshake from the tub, transfer to a glass, top with crushed cookies. serve

BANANA PEANUT BUTTER MILKSHAKE

Serving size 1-2 **Prep time 3 mins**

INGREDIENTS

- 200g vanilla ice cream
- 100ml milk
- 4 tbsp peanut butter
- 1 ripe banana, sliced

Topping:
- Chopped peanuts

DIRECTIONS

1. Place all ingredients into empty tub in the order listed, (except topping).
2. Place tub in outer bowl, install the Paddle onto outer bowl lid, and lock the lid assembly on the outer bowl. Place bowl assembly on motor base and twist the handle right to raise the platform and lock in place. Select MILKSHAKE.
3. Remove the milkshake from the tub, transfer to a glass, top with Chopped peanuts. serve.

Drizzle a swirl of caramel sauce over the top of the milkshake. You can also add a pinch of sea salt to the caramel for a salted caramel twist.

MINTY GREEN DELIGHT MILKSHAKE

Serving size 1-2   **Prep time** 3 mins

INGREDIENTS

- 1/4 tsp peppermint extract
- 100ml milk
- 200g vanilla ice cream
- 2 to 3 drops green food coloring

Topping:
- Melted chocolate
- Whipped cream
- Mint leaves

DIRECTIONS

1. Place all ingredients into empty tub in the order listed, (except toppings).
2. Place tub in outer bowl, install the Paddle onto outer bowl lid, and lock the lid assembly on the outer bowl. Place bowl assembly on motor base and twist the handle right to raise the platform and lock in place. Select MILKSHAKE.
3. Remove the milkshake from the tub, transfer to a glass, top with Whipped cream, Mint leaves, and melted chocolate. serve.

COCONUT PINEAPPLE MILKSHAKE

Serving size 1-2   **Prep time** 3 mins

INGREDIENTS

- 100ml coconut milk
- 200g vanilla ice cream
- 100g Pineapple chunks

Topping:
- Whipped cream
- Pineapple chunks

DIRECTIONS

1. Place all ingredients into empty tub in the order listed, (except toppings).
2. Place tub in outer bowl, install the Paddle onto outer bowl lid, and lock the lid assembly on the outer bowl. Place bowl assembly on motor base and twist the handle right to raise the platform and lock in place. Select MILKSHAKE.
3. Remove the milkshake from the tub, transfer to a glass, top with Whipped cream, and pineapple chunks. serve.

CARAMEL COFFEE MILKSHAKE

Serving size 1-2   Prep time 3 mins

INGREDIENTS

- 200g vanilla ice cream
- 100ml milk
- 2 tbsp instant coffee
- 2 tbsp cocoa powder
- 2 tbsp caramel syrup

Topping:
- Whipped cream
- Cocoa powder
- Chocolate syrup

DIRECTIONS

1. Place all ingredients into empty tub in the order listed, (except toppings).
2. Place tub in outer bowl, install the Paddle onto outer bowl lid, and lock the lid assembly on the outer bowl. Place bowl assembly on motor base and twist the handle right to raise the platform and lock in place. Select MILKSHAKE.
3. Remove the milkshake from the tub, transfer to a glass, top with Whipped cream, chocolate syrup and cocoa powder. serve.

APPLE PIE MILKSHAKE

Serving size 1-2   Prep time 3 mins

INGREDIENTS

- 100ml milk
- 200g vanilla ice cream
- 1/2 tsp cinnamon
- 100g apple pie filling or 1 (100g) apple pie slice

Topping:
- Whipped cream
- Caramel sauce

DIRECTIONS

1. Place all ingredients into empty tub in the order listed, (except toppings).
2. Place tub in outer bowl, install the Paddle onto outer bowl lid, and lock the lid assembly on the outer bowl. Place bowl assembly on motor base and twist the handle right to raise the platform and lock in place. Select MILKSHAKE.
3. Remove the milkshake from the tub, transfer to a glass, top with Whipped cream, and caramel sauce. serve.

VANILLA CHERRY MILKSHAKE

Serving size 1-2   Prep time 3 mins

INGREDIENTS

- 200g vanilla ice cream
- 100ml milk
- 130g cherries pitted, halved

Topping:
- Whipped cream
- Sprinkles

DIRECTIONS

1. Place all ingredients into empty tub in the order listed, (except **toppings**)
2. Place tub in outer bowl, install the Paddle onto outer bowl lid, and lock the lid assembly on the outer bowl. Place bowl assembly on motor base and twist the handle right to raise the platform and lock in place. Select MILKSHAKE.
3. Remove the milkshake from the tub, transfer to a glass, top with Whipped cream, and Sprinkles. serve.

WHITE CHOCOLATE AVOCADO MILKSHAKE

Serving size 1-2   Prep time 3 mins

INGREDIENTS

- 200g vanilla ice cream
- 100ml milk
- 40g white chocolate chips
- 1 ripe avocado, peeled, pitted

Topping:
- Whipped cream
- Caramel sauce

DIRECTIONS

1. Place all ingredients into empty tub in the order listed, (except toppings)
2. Place tub in outer bowl, install the Paddle onto outer bowl lid, and lock the lid assembly on the outer bowl. Place bowl assembly on motor base and twist the handle right to raise the platform and lock in place. Select MILKSHAKE.
3. Remove the milkshake from the tub, transfer to a glass, top with more white chocolate chips. serve.

MIXED BERRIES MILKSHAKE

Serving size **1-2**   **Prep time** **2 mins**

INGREDIENTS

- 200g vanilla ice cream
- 100ml milk
- 120g mixed berries such as (strawberries, blueberries, raspberries)

Topping:
- Whipped cream

DIRECTIONS

1. Place all ingredients into empty tub in the order listed, (except topping).
2. Place tub in outer bowl, install the Paddle onto outer bowl lid, and lock the lid assembly on the outer bowl. Place bowl assembly on motor base and twist the handle right to raise the platform and lock in place. Select MILKSHAKE.
3. Remove the milkshake from the tub, transfer to a glass, top with Whipped cream. serve.

Sorbet

GRAPE SORBET

Serving size 4   **Prep time** 2 mins

INGREDIENTS

- 450g grapes
- 50g brown sugar
- juice of 1 small lemon

DIRECTIONS

1. Fill an empty tub with grapes. Next, add the lemon juice and sugar. Press the grapes below the MAX FILL line with potato masher. Place lid on tub and freeze for 24 hours.
2. After 24 hours, remove the tub from the freezer and remove lid from tub, and let it thaw for 5 minutes. Place the tub in the Creami and lock the lid. Select SORBET.
3. Once processing is complete, remove sorbet from tub and serve immediately.

PLUM BERRY SORBET

Serving size 4   **Prep time** 6 mins

INGREDIENTS

- 200g fresh plums, pitted and chopped
- 2 tsp honey
- 200g fresh or frozen mixed berries (such as raspberries, blueberries, or strawberries)

DIRECTIONS

1. In a blender, add plums and berries blend until they're finely pureed. Add in the honey.
2. Pour mixture into Ninja Creami tub container, ensuring it does not go over the max fill line. Place lid on tub and freeze for 24 hours.
3. After 24 hours, remove the tub from the freezer and remove lid from tub, and let it thaw for 5 minutes. Place the tub in the Creami and lock the lid. Select SORBET.
4. Once processing is complete, remove sorbet from tub and serve immediately.

LEMON MINT SORBET

Serving size 4   **Prep time 7 mins**

INGREDIENTS

- 100g sugar
- 210ml hot water, 60-70°C
- 100ml lemon juice
- 1/2 tsp peppermint extract or 2 tbsp chopped fresh mint leaves

DIRECTIONS

1. In a large bowl, whisk together sugar, peppermint extract and warm water until sugar is dissolved. Add lemon juice and whisk until fully combined.
2. Pour base into an empty tub. Place lid on tub and freeze for 24 hours.
3. After 24 hours, remove the tub from the freezer and remove lid from tub, and let it thaw for 5 minutes. Place the tub in the Creami and lock the lid. Select SORBET.
4. Once the process is finished, sorbet is ready to enjoy.

WATERMELON KIWI SORBET

Serving size 4   **Prep time 10 mins**

INGREDIENTS

- 200g watermelon cubed with seeds removed
- 200g kiwi, peeled and chopped
- 100g sugar
- 1 tsp lemon juice

DIRECTIONS

1. In a blender, add watermelon, lemon juice, sugar and kiwi blend until they're finely pureed.
2. Pour mixture into Ninja Creami tub container, ensuring it does not go over the max fill line. Place lid on tub and freeze for 24 hours.
3. After 24 hours, remove the tub from the freezer and remove lid from tub, and let it thaw for 5 minutes. Place the tub in the Creami and lock the lid. Select SORBET.
4. Once processing is complete, remove sorbet from tub and serve immediately.

MANGO SORBET

Serving size 4   **Prep time 10 mins**

INGREDIENTS

- 400g fresh mangoes, peeled and chopped
- 75g caster sugar
- 1 tbsp lemon juice

DIRECTIONS

1. In a blender add mango, sugar and lemon juice. Blend until smooth.
2. Pour mixture into Ninja Creami tub container, ensuring it does not go over the max fill line. Place lid on tub and freeze for 24 hours.
3. After 24 hours, remove the tub from the freezer and remove lid from tub, and let it thaw for 5 minutes. Place the tub in the Creami and lock the lid. Select SORBET.
4. Once processing is complete, remove sorbet from tub and serve immediately.

CLEMENTINE SORBET

Serving size 4   **Prep time 2 mins**

INGREDIENTS

- 50g sugar
- 300ml clementine juice
- 100ml hot water, 60-70°C

DIRECTIONS

1. In a large bowl, whisk together sugar, and warm water until sugar is dissolved. Add clementine juice and whisk until fully combined.
2. Pour base into an empty tub. Place lid on tub and freeze for 24 hours.
3. After 24 hours, remove the tub from the freezer and remove lid from tub, and let it thaw for 5 minutes. Place the tub in the Creami and lock the lid. Select SORBET.
4. Once the process is finished, sorbet is ready to enjoy.

BLOOD ORANGE SORBET

Serving size 4   **Prep time 10 mins**

INGREDIENTS

- 100g sugar
- 2 tbsp honey
- 150ml hot water, 60-70°C
- 160ml blood orange juice

DIRECTIONS

1. In a large bowl, whisk together sugar, honey, and warm water until sugar is dissolved. Add orange juice and whisk until fully combined.
2. Pour base into an empty tub. Place lid on tub and freeze for 24 hours.
3. After 24 hours, remove the tub from the freezer and remove lid from tub, and let it thaw for 5 minutes. Place the tub in the Creami and lock the lid. Select SORBET.
4. Once the process is finished, sorbet is ready to enjoy.

PINEAPPLE ORANGE SORBET

Serving size 4   **Prep time 4 mins**

INGREDIENTS

- 200g canned pineapple drained
- 200ml fresh orange juice
- 2 tbsp icing sugar

DIRECTIONS

1. In a blender, add all ingredients. Blend until smooth.
2. Pour base into an empty tub. Place lid on tub and freeze for 24 hours.
3. After 24 hours, remove the tub from the freezer and remove lid from tub, and let it thaw for 5 minutes. Place the tub in the Creami and lock the lid. Select SORBET.
4. Once the process is finished, sorbet is ready to enjoy.

RASPBERRY AND REDCURRANT SORBET

Serving size 4   Prep time 5 mins

INGREDIENTS

- 200g raspberries
- 200g redcurrants
- 125g icing sugar

DIRECTIONS

1. In a blender, add all ingredients. Blend until smooth.
2. Pour base into an empty tub. Place lid on tub and freeze for 24 hours.
3. After 24 hours, remove the tub from the freezer and remove lid from tub, and let it thaw for 5 minutes. Place the tub in the Creami and lock the lid. Select SORBET.
4. Once the process is finished, sorbet is ready to enjoy.

RHUBARB AND STRAWBERRY SORBET

Serving size 4   Prep time 10 mins

INGREDIENTS

- 150g chopped rhubarb
- 100g sugar
- 1/4 tsp salt
- 1 tbsp lemon juice
- 150ml water
- 200g strawberries, hulled and chopped

DIRECTIONS

1. In a large saucepan over medium heat, add rhubarb, sugar, salt, lemon and water. Simmer for 11 minutes until rhubarb softened. Let cool.
2. In a blender, add rhubarb mixture and strawberries, blend until smooth.
3. Pour base into an empty tub. Place lid on tub and freeze for 24 hours.
4. After 24 hours, remove the tub from the freezer and remove lid from tub, and let it thaw for 5 minutes. Place the tub in the Creami and lock the lid. Select SORBET.
5. Once the process is finished, sorbet is ready to enjoy.

STRAWBERRY BALSAMIC SORBET

Serving size 4   **Prep time 10 mins**

INGREDIENTS

- 450g fresh Strawberries, sliced
- 75g caster sugar
- 75g hot water, 60-70°C
- tbsp balsamic vinegar

DIRECTIONS

1. In a large bowl, add the strawberries and sugar and mash together with a fork. Stir in water and balsamic vinegar, whisk until smooth.
2. Pour base into an empty tub. Place lid on tub and freeze for 24 hours.
3. After 24 hours, remove the tub from the freezer and remove lid from tub, and let it thaw for 5 minutes. Place the tub in the Creami and lock the lid. Select SORBET.
4. Once the process is finished, sorbet is ready to enjoy.

CHOCOLATE ORANGE SORBET

Serving size 4   **Prep time 15 mins**

INGREDIENTS

- 100ml water
- 400ml fresh orange juice
- 1 tsp orange zest
- 100g caster sugar
- 50g cocoa powder

DIRECTIONS

1. Place water, orange juice sugar, orange zest and cocoa powder into a small saucepan, heat until just simmering, whisk until fully combined and sugar is dissolved.
2. Pour base into an empty tub. Place lid on tub and freeze for 24 hours.
3. After 24 hours, remove the tub from the freezer and remove lid from tub, and let it thaw for 5 minutes. Place the tub in the Creami and lock the lid. Select SORBET.
4. Once the process is finished, sorbet is ready to enjoy.

KIWI LIME SORBET

Serving size 4   **Prep time** 10 mins

INGREDIENTS

- 400g kiwi, peeled and chopped
- 50g sugar
- 80ml water
- 1 lime juice

DIRECTIONS

1. In a blender, add sugar, water, lime and kiwi blend until smooth.
2. Pour mixture into Ninja Creami tub container, ensuring it does not go over the max fill line. Place lid on tub and freeze for 24 hours.
3. After 24 hours, remove the tub from the freezer and remove lid from tub, and let it thaw for 5 minutes. Place the tub in the Creami and lock the lid. Select SORBET.
4. Once processing is complete, remove sorbet from tub and serve immediately.

GINGER AND ORANGE SORBET

Serving size 4   **Prep time** 10 mins

INGREDIENTS

- 400ml orange juice
- 50g icing sugar
- 1 tsp grated fresh ginger

DIRECTIONS

1. In a bowl add all ingredients and mix until sugar dissolved.
2. Pour mixture into Ninja Creami tub container, ensuring it does not go over the max fill line. Place lid on tub and freeze for 24 hours.
3. After 24 hours, remove the tub from the freezer and remove lid from tub, and let it thaw for 5 minutes. Place the tub in the Creami and lock the lid. Select SORBET.
4. Once processing is complete, remove sorbet from tub and serve immediately.

PEACH SORBET

Serving size 4   **Prep time 10 mins**

INGREDIENTS

- 400g canned peaches
- 100ml canned peaches juice
- 2 tbsp lemon juice

DIRECTIONS

1. In a blender, add all ingredients and **blend until smooth**.
2. Pour mixture into Ninja Creami tub container, **ensuring it does not go over the max** fill line. Place lid on tub and freeze for 24 hours.
3. After 24 hours, remove the tub from the freezer and remove lid from tub, and let it thaw for 5 minutes. Place the tub in the Creami and lock the lid. Select SORBET.
4. Once processing is complete, remove sorbet from tub and serve immediately.

WATERMELON BASIL SORBET

Serving size 4   **Prep time 5 mins**

INGREDIENTS

- 400g watermelon cubed with seeds removed
- 100g sugar
- 1 tsp lemon juice
- 2 tbsp finely chopped basil leaves

DIRECTIONS

1. In a blender, add all ingredients and blend until smooth.
2. Pour mixture into Ninja Creami tub container, ensuring it does not **go over the max** fill line. Place lid on tub and freeze for 24 hours.
3. After 24 hours, remove the tub from the freezer and remove lid from tub, and let it thaw for 5 minutes. Place the tub in the Creami and lock the lid. Select SORBET.
4. Once processing is complete, remove sorbet from tub and serve immediately.

TROPICAL FRUIT SORBET

Serving size 4   **Prep time 10 mins**

INGREDIENTS

* 150g ripe mango chuncks
* 150g fresh or frozen pineapple chuncks
* 1 passion fruit pulp
* 50g Sugar

DIRECTIONS

1. In a blender, add all ingredients and blend until smooth.
2. Pour mixture into Ninja Creami tub container, ensuring it does not go over the max fill line. Place lid on tub and freeze for 24 hours.
3. After 24 hours, remove the tub from the freezer and remove lid from tub, and let it thaw for 5 minutes. Place the tub in the Creami and lock the lid. Select SORBET.
4. Once processing is complete, remove sorbet from tub and serve immediately.

SUNSHINE SORBET

Serving size 4   **Prep time 10 mins**

INGREDIENTS

* 80ml orange juice
* 150g mango chunks
* 100g chopped peaches
* 100g chopped apricots
* 50g sugar
* 1 tbsp fresh lemon juice

DIRECTIONS

1. In a blender, add all ingredients. Blend **until smooth.**
2. Pour base into an empty tub. Place lid on tub and freeze for 24 hours.
3. After 24 hours, remove the tub from the freezer and remove lid from tub, and let it thaw for 5 minutes. Place the tub in the Creami and lock the lid. Select SORBET.
4. Once the process is finished, sorbet is ready to enjoy.

RASPBERRY SORBET

Serving size 4   **Prep time 5 mins**

INGREDIENTS

- 400g fresh or frozen raspberries
- 50g sugar
- 60ml water
- 1 tsp lemon juice

DIRECTIONS

1. In a blender, add all ingredients. Blend until smooth.
2. Pour base into an empty tub. Place lid on tub and freeze for 24 hours.
3. After 24 hours, remove the tub from the freezer and remove lid from tub, and let it thaw for 5 minutes. Place the tub in the Creami and lock the lid. Select SORBET.
4. Once the process is finished, sorbet is ready to enjoy.

Raspberry Pomegranate Sorbet: Mix in pomegranate juice or arils with the raspberries for a vibrant and antioxidant-rich sorbet.

COCONUT SORBET

Serving size 4   **Prep time 5 mins**

INGREDIENTS

- 200ml Unsweetened Coconut Milk
- 200ml Unsweetened Coconut Water
- 100g Sugar
- 40g Shredded Coconut

DIRECTIONS

1. In a bowl, add all ingredients. Whisk until smooth.
2. Pour base into an empty tub. Place lid on tub and freeze for 24 hours.
3. After 24 hours, remove the tub from the freezer and remove lid from tub, and let it thaw for 5 minutes. Place the tub in the Creami and lock the lid. Select SORBET.
4. Once the process is finished, sorbet is ready to enjoy.

APRICOT SORBET

Serving size 4   **Prep time 5 mins**

INGREDIENTS

- 250g apricots, chopped and pitted
- 100g canned peaches
- 100ml canned peaches juice

DIRECTIONS

1. In a blender, add all ingredients. Blend until smooth.
2. Pour base into an empty tub. Place lid on tub and freeze for 24 hours.
3. After 24 hours, remove the tub from the freezer and remove lid from tub, and let it thaw for 5 minutes. Place the tub in the Creami and lock the lid. Select SORBET.
4. Once the process is finished, sorbet is ready to enjoy.

BLUEBERRY HONEY SORBET

Serving size 4   **Prep time 5 mins**

INGREDIENTS

- 400g fresh or frozen blueberries
- 50g honey
- 60ml water
- 1 tsp lemon juice

DIRECTIONS

1. In a blender, add all ingredients. Blend until smooth.
2. Pour base into an empty tub. Place lid on tub and freeze for 24 hours.
3. After 24 hours, remove the tub from the freezer and remove lid from tub, and let it thaw for 5 minutes. Place the tub in the Creami and lock the lid. Select SORBET.
4. Once the process is finished, sorbet is ready to enjoy.

YOGURT LIME SORBET

Serving size 4   **Prep time 8 mins**

INGREDIENTS

- 100g sugar
- 100ml water
- 250g yogurt
- 1 tsp lime zest
- 3 tbsp fresh lime juice
- ½ tsp vanilla extract

DIRECTIONS

1. In a blender, add all ingredients. Blend until smooth.
2. Pour base into an empty tub. Place lid on tub and freeze for 24 hours.
3. After 24 hours, remove the tub from the freezer and remove lid from tub, and let it thaw for 5 minutes. Place the tub in the Creami and lock the lid. Select SORBET.
4. Once the process is finished, sorbet is ready to enjoy.

STRAWBERRY MANGO SORBET

Serving size 4   **Prep time 5 mins**

INGREDIENTS

- 200g fresh or frozen strawberries, chopped
- 200g fresh or frozen ripe mango chunks
- 30g sugar
- 50ml water
- 1 tsp lemon juice

DIRECTIONS

1. In a blender, add all ingredients. Blend until smooth.
2. Pour base into an empty tub. Place lid on tub and freeze for 24 hours.
3. After 24 hours, remove the tub from the freezer and remove lid from tub, and let it thaw for 5 minutes. Place the tub in the Creami and lock the lid. Select SORBET.
4. Once the process is finished, sorbet is ready to enjoy.

Index

Ice Cream

Smoothie Bowl

Milkshake

Sorbet

Printed in Great Britain
by Amazon

55368197R00044